The Franciscan Intellectual Tradition

Washington Theological Union
Symposium Papers
2001

The Franciscan Intellectual Tradition

Washington Theological Union Symposium Papers
2001

Edited by
Elise Saggau, O.S.F.

The Franciscan Institute
St. Bonaventure University
St. Bonaventure, New York
2002

CFIT/ESC-OFM SERIES
NUMBER 1

The articles in this book were originally presented
at a symposium sponsored by the Franciscan Center at
Washington Theological Union, Washington, DC,
May 25-27, 2001.
This publication is the first in a series of documents
resulting from the work of the
Commission on the Franciscan Intellectual Tradition of the
English-speaking Conference of the
Order of Friars Minor.
(CFIT/ESC-OFM)

Cover design: Jennifer L. Davis

ISBN
1-57659-180-8

Library of Congress Control Number
2001119689

Printed and bound in the United States of America
BookMasters, Inc.
Mansfield, Ohio

TABLE OF CONTENTS

FOREWORD

In March of 2000 the English Speaking Conference of the Order of Friars Minor (ESC-OFM) invited representatives of the study centers in the jurisdiction of the conference to a special meeting to discuss the state of Franciscan intellectual formation, research, and publication. During this meeting, many concerns surfaced relative to a renewed commitment to fostering the educational resources of the Conference. The ESC members responded by establishing a Task Force charged with providing a plan of action to the ESC the following year.[1]

When the Task Force submitted its report and recommendations one year later, its members were invited to serve as a Commission on the Franciscan Intellectual Tradition (CFIT) with a five-year mandate to work under the auspices of the ESC-OFM. The Task Force Report was then published with the title "The Franciscan Intellectual Tradition Project."[2] Once the members were assigned to the Commission, they addressed the question of dissemination of on-going work. The Franciscan Institute offered its publication services to organize publications of materials pertinent to the Commission's efforts in a series designated for that purpose. All such publications are the joint responsibility of the ESC-OFM and the press of the Franciscan Institute.

With the announcement of the 2001 Washington Theological Union Symposium, "The Franciscan Intellectual Tradition: Is It Meaningful Today?," we could see that the papers of this symposium would be the first public discussion of the themes the Task Force/Commission promoted in its meetings and report. The evident high interest and attendance at the Symposium gave testimony to the timeliness of the topic and the readiness of Franciscan teachers,

---

[1]Members of the Task Force were: Joseph Chinnici, O.F.M., Dean, Franciscan School of Theology, Berkeley; Margaret Carney, O.S.F., Director, Franciscan Institute, St. Bonaventure University; F. Edward Coughlin, O.F.M., Secretary, Holy Name Province, New York; Ilia Delio, O.S.F., Director, Franciscan Center, Washington Theological Union; William Short, O.F.M., Franciscan School of Theology, Berkeley; Cyprian Rosen, O.F.M. Cap., Capuchin Franciscan Scholar; Austin McCormick, O.F.M., Provincial Minister, England; Pierre Brunette, O.F.M., Provincial Minister, Montreal, Canada.

[2]The report was published by the Franciscan Publishers of Pulaski, WI, and is available through the Franciscan Institute.

students, and leaders to enter into sustained conversation about these questions and concerns.

This publication is thus the first of a documentation series that will publish the results of the work of CFIT/ESC-OFM. The members of the bodies that have produced the initial results and publications are the first to acknowledge the importance and the satisfaction of participation in this international and collaborative ongoing colloquium. The work of Ilia Delio, O.S.F., who organized the 2001 Symposium on this theme and engaged the brilliant panel of lecturers whose papers are printed here, was a major step in widening the circle of this conversation. We hope that the readers of these materials will be well served by our mutual efforts.

Margaret Carney, O.S.F., Director
The Franciscan Institute

PREFACE

A wonderful contemporary experience is the retrieval, indeed the renaissance, of Franciscan scholarship available in symposia, workshops, and a host of books and journals. As a student in the mid-1950s, when I first came to read the Franciscan tradition, only a few cherished classics were available. The works of Jorgenson, Felder, the graphic genius of Leonard Von Matt, and the ever-delightful Chesterton come to mind. At that time I was introduced to biographies of St. Francis and folklore about the tradition, with the hope that these would respond to my searching queries. They did not. I—and others—wanted more. Sound scholarly studies, critical historiography, systematic theology rooted in scriptural, philosophical, and linguistic advances were soon offered us in the second half of the next decade. Little did we know then that the splendid scholars of that day—Philotheus Boehner, Kajetan Esser, Allan Wolter, the two Brady brothers, Ignatius and Mel, not to mention the ecumenical contribution of many Anglican scholars, most notably Bishop John Moorman, would soon create a strong foundation for this present age. Not only did the scholars of the 50s and 60s spark a vibrant revival of first-rate Franciscan scholarship, they also made their scholarship accessible for eager readers on the popular level.

For the past forty years, their progeny have worked long and hard and have further probed, developed, translated, and made available deeper riches of this ancient, yet fertile tradition. Indeed, they have gone further and deeper in exploring the relationship of past to present for import and future promise. While still in its initial stages, this exploring of the past in light of the contemporary has established a launching pad for what might well be described as a third generation of Franciscan studies. Nor is that study now limited solely to members of the religious institutes of the Franciscan family. Other scholars, Catholic, Protestant and, yes, Jewish, are now numbered among significant commentators on the Franciscan tradition.

Of the many remarkable directions set out in Vatican II, the call to religious institutes of women and men to return to the charism of their particular founder has yielded a great amount of scholarship in history and theology. This is evident in a broad range of monographs in the rich traditions of mendicant and monastic families—Augustinian,

Benedictine, Carmelite, Dominican, and Franciscan, both male and female. They, coupled with the excellent scholarship in the Ignatian tradition and the fruitful ecumenical retrieval in Patristic studies, have made this current age one of extraordinary promise in the development of the spirituality characteristic of each family, as well as providing new paths for exploration in contemporary systematic theology. In the Franciscan tradition, this is particularly evident in the theology of Christ and the theology of creation. What is so extraordinary—and I fervently hope will become ordinary—is that each family now intentionally nourishes eager students, both members and other interested learners, in a sound and scholarly introduction to the best of each tradition. This volume bears witness to that.

One source of that scholarship is the Franciscan Center, now under the imaginative direction of Dr. Ilia Delio, O.S.F., who serves with the noted Franciscan scholar, Dr. Dominic Monti, O.F.M., professor of church history at the Washington Theological Union. Ever since Dr. Anthony Carrozzo, O.F.M., then Provincial Minister, and the friars of the Province of the Most Holy Name of the Order of Friars Minor, endowed the Franciscan Center at the Washington Theological Union, it has brought together annually scholars to break open a specific vein of Franciscan studies. This effort, however, is not (and should not be) the work of one institution. It is made possible through generous cooperation and publishing by the Franciscan Institute of St. Bonaventure University, the venerable founding institute of Franciscan scholarship in the United States. In addition, the contributors to this volume include scholars from other North American graduate institutions of theology and spirituality: the Catholic Theological Union of Chicago and the Franciscan School of Theology, Berkeley, California.

The scholarship in this volume on the Franciscan intellectual tradition represents an array of gifted North American thinkers who have addressed the relationship of past tradition and contemporary issues. They continue the important task of bringing historical knowledge, critical acumen, and theological imagination to a dialogue of the past with our contemporary age. Drs. Zachary Hayes, O.F.M., Kenan Osborne, O.F.M., Joseph Chinnici, O.F.M., and Dominic Monti, O.F.M., now constitute well over a hundred years of significant, long-term contribution to theology and history and particularly to Franciscan theology and history. Dr. Ilia Delio, O.S.F., Dr. Mary Beth Ingham,

C.S.J., and Diane Tomkinson, O.S.F., are now taking up the scholarly task anew. It is especially encouraging to see women enter this field of study since so many have lived the Franciscan tradition with great imagination and authenticity. The combination of senior and younger scholars gives a certain freshness and imaginative edge to these important studies. Each splendidly contributes to this volume on the intellectual tradition and its meaning for contemporary life.

We are both blessed and deeply appreciative to present their work to the larger family of readers and scholars who will benefit from it.

Vincent Cushing, O.F.M.
Washington Theological Union,
Solemnity of St. Francis, 2001

Chapter One

THE FRANCISCAN INTELLECTUAL TRADITION: CONTEMPORARY CONCERNS

Ilia Delio, O.S.F.

Introduction

In his provocative work, *The Analogical Imagination*, David Tracy confronts the reader with a challenging question. He writes: "In a culture of pluralism must each religious tradition finally either dissolve into some lowest common denominator or accept a marginal existence as one interesting but purely private option?"[1] Although Tracy will argue for the public role of Christian theology in a pluralistic world, the same question could be applied to a specific religious tradition within Christianity such as the Franciscan tradition. We may ask, in our post-modern culture,[2] must the Franciscan tradition either dissolve into some lowest common denominator or accept a marginal existence as one interesting but private option? The question is startling when one considers the fact that Francis of Assisi was anything but a private person. His charism and transformation into the iconic figure of Christ had far-reaching effects on the Church and society in the Middle Ages. From the charism of this one individual sprang a whole movement that would culminate in a tradition known as the Franciscan tradition. But

---

[1]David Tracy, *The Analogical Imagination: Christian Theology and the Culture of Pluralism* (New York: Crossroad, 1981), xi.

[2]Postmodernism is a complex term that describes the contemporary philosophical and cultural milieu. Coined in the 1930s, the term "postmodern" is used to describe the historical transition from modernity to a period beyond modernity, namely, postmodernity. Whereas modernity emphasized objective, logical thinking, as well as a universal morality and law, postmodernism indicates there is no transcendence in reality; rather, all knowledge is derived from the self who interprets reality. Thus, there is no single, universal worldview. Postmodernism celebrates the local and particular at the expense of the universal and emphasizes a respect for difference. For an introduction to postmodernism, see Stanley J. Grenz, *A Primer on Postmodernism* (Grand Rapids: William B. Eerdmans, 1996), 39-56.

1

what exactly is this tradition and what is it as an intellectual tradition? Who are the bearers of this tradition and what is its purpose? Do we know enough of what the Franciscan intellectual tradition is to ask if it can be a public voice in the Church and world today?

When we hear the Franciscan tradition described as "intellectual" we are taken aback, since the word itself seems antithetical to the spirit of Francis. Certainly, for Francis and Clare, intellectual learning was not held in high esteem. To follow Christ and to pursue a life of poverty meant that books were not to be accrued either individually or communally nor should one pursue academic study because it risked engendering intellectual pride.[3] But is the Franciscan intellectual tradition about book learning or is it a set of values, theologically informed, that comprise a distinct view of the world, one that takes as its basis the theological intuitions of Francis of Assisi? Although it would be impossible to answer this question in a short amount of time, I do not think we can easily identify contemporary concerns about the tradition unless we know what the tradition is.

What I would like to do, therefore, is to "break open" the meaning of the Franciscan intellectual tradition. First, I would like to explore the meaning of the word "tradition" and then to ask, is the Franciscan intellectual tradition really a tradition integral to Franciscan life? I would like to suggest that the Franciscan intellectual tradition arose out of the theological intuitions of Francis and initially had a profound influence on the shape of Franciscan evangelical life. In light of this, I will briefly examine the synthesis of evangelical theology and lived experience as it emerged in the writings of Celano and culminated in the writings of Bonaventure. I will suggest that the synthesis of theology and lived experience formulated by these writers eventually collapsed leaving the Franciscan intellectual tradition to develop as an elite school of thought divorced from the tradition of Franciscan life. That is, the Franciscan intellectual tradition developed as a tradition within a tradition. In the latter part of my talk, I will discuss recent efforts to renew the Franciscan intellectual tradition in light of Franciscan evangelical life. It is in the context of lived experience, I believe, that the intellectual tradition finds its deepest meaning.

---

[3]Leslie Knox, "Clare of Assisi and Learning: A Foundation for Intellectual Life within the Franciscan Second Order," *Cord*, 46.4 (July/Aug. 1996): 172. Although Knox is speaking about the intellectual tradition among the Poor Clares, the same statement can easily be applied to Francis of Assisi.

Is the "Franciscan Intellectual Tradition" a Tradition?

Tradition comes from the Latin *traditio*, the noun of the verb *tradere* meaning to transmit, to deliver. Used as a term of ratification in Roman law, the word *tradere* meant to hand over an object with the intention of parting with it on the one hand and of acquiring it on the other. A good simile would be that of a relay race where the runners, spaced at intervals, pass an object from one to the other, for example, a baton or torch.[4] Although the word tradition implies conservatism, it is more than retaining the past; rather, it is the continual presence of a spirit and of a moral attitude.[5] Yves Congar has described tradition as a "spontaneous assimilation of the past in understanding the present, without a break in the continuity of a society's life, and without considering the past as outmoded."[6] Perhaps we might say that tradition enables the continuity of values/ideas as the past yields to the present. What links one generation to another is the principle of identity, which is inherent to tradition and which tradition strives to maintain.

Before examining the meaning of the Franciscan intellectual tradition, I would like to begin with a preliminary question, namely, what characterizes a tradition? Cicero once claimed that tradition is like a second nature.[7] This leads us to suggest that tradition is integral to identity. When we think of the Franciscan tradition we think of a core set of values such as poverty, conversion, and peacemaking, which have been maintained in an identifiable way through rules and customs passed down through succeeding generations. In light of the Franciscan tradition, we can say that every authentic tradition has certain features. First, there is a core of fundamental values and beliefs that are particular to the tradition. Next, there are witnesses to the tradition, those in whom the set of beliefs have taken root and become visible in such a way that the tradition has formed a culture. Clifford Geertz states that cultures are socially established structures of meaning in which human actions gain their meanings.[8] Traditions give rise to cultures because

---

[4]Yves Congar, *The Meaning of Tradition*, trans. A. N. Woodrow (New York: Hawthorn Books, 1964), 14 – 15.

[5]Congar, 7.

[6]Congar, 8.

[7]Cicero, *De Finibus Bonorum et Malorum*, 5.25.74, trans. H. Rackham, Leob Classical Library (Cambridge: Harvard University Press, 1983), 476.

[8]Clifford Geertz, *The Interpretation of Cultures* (New York: Basic Books, 1973), 12-13.

they give rise to meaningful lives. The recipients of a tradition are those who bear witness to its particular meaning. It is they to whom the future of the tradition is entrusted insofar as they remain faithful to the identity of the tradition. What makes a tradition a tradition, therefore, is the reception and transmission of a core set of values/beliefs that shape a particular culture in such a way that the self-identity of the tradition is maintained from past to present by those who bear witness to it.

Delwin Brown states that traditions are creative insofar as they maintain a dynamic interface between culture and canon. Canons, he says, are reasonably defined "spaces," bodies of material—texts, doctrines, symbols, rituals, or combinations of these—within which and with which the negotiation is conducted.[9] A tradition that lives within canonical space can grow creatively as long as fidelity to the core of the tradition is maintained. He writes:

> The creativity of a tradition is the tensive character of the life lived within, and sometimes against, its boundaries. The viability of a tradition is the vastness of its collected resources, unified enough to sustain needed continuity and diverse enough to create something new for new times. The power of a tradition is the worth of its space, the productivity of its complementary and competing voices, as it progresses through the novelties of history. The dynamism of a tradition is its contestability and therefore its perpetual contest. The relevance of a tradition is its contemporaneity, what it brings to and receives from the discourse of truth in every age. But the life of a tradition, its vitality as a real way of being in the world, is the assumption of its resources as one's own. Tradition is canon lived—the negotiation of corporate and personal identities within canonical space.[10]

Canons, therefore, are the spaces within which adherents continuously and repeatedly negotiate who they are. Tradition is canon made existential, canon lived. Negotiating identity in relationship to a canon means construing the canon as a framework in terms of which

[9]Delwin Brown, *Boundaries of Our Habitations: Tradition and Theological Construction* (Albany: State University of New York Press, 1994), 90.
[10]Brown, 89.

one understands oneself, one's social and natural world, and one's place in it.[11]

When we apply these ideas of tradition to the Franciscan *intellectual* tradition we are faced with some challenging questions. First, if this is truly a tradition, what are the core values or set of beliefs that define it? What is its identity and how is it in creative tension with the past? To whom are these beliefs entrusted, that is, who are the bearers of this tradition? Finally, what are the canons of this tradition that make it meaningful? What guides the Franciscan intellectual tradition and enables it to grow while remaining faithful to its core values? Of these questions, the first can be answered with some assuredness. A brief look at the tradition enables us to identify key themes that, since the time of Francis, have been held as fundamental themes in the tradition. These include an emphasis on divine love and freedom, the primacy of Christ, the centrality of the Incarnation and, in particular Christ crucified, the sacramentality of creation, the goodness of the world, the human person as image of God, an emphasis on poverty and humility, and the development of *affectus*. While this list does not exhaust the tradition, it highlights its key characteristics.

The remaining questions are more difficult to answer. We may assume that Franciscans are the bearers of the intellectual tradition and that the canon of the tradition is Franciscan life but there seems to be no real connection today between the Franciscan intellectual tradition and Franciscan life. Indeed, the intellectual tradition seems to follow a trajectory that deviates from the life, one guided by medieval scholastic thought. This leads us to ask, is the Franciscan intellectual tradition a tradition unto its own?

Tradition and Evangelical Life

While we may consider the Franciscan intellectual tradition as somewhat nebulous, at least with regard to the life, there is every reason to believe that it originated in the core values of Francis and Clare. Although the word "intellectual" connotes book learning and does not appropriately describe the distinct values of Francis and Clare, we can at the same time profess that neither Francis nor Clare were simply

---

[11]Brown, 90.

pragmatic Christians.[12] They were not savants in the intellectual sense but their lives were theological by definition. Bernard McGinn has identified Francis as a vernacular theologian. This means that the authority of Francis's theological voice emerged from his experience of God.[13] Clare, too, could easily be defined as a vernacular theologian, one in whom *scientia* gave way to *sapientia*.[14] McGinn describes vernacular theology as a third type of medieval theology (alongside that of monastic and scholastic theology) whose distinguishing mark is linguistic expression in the medieval vernacular tongues.[15] The idea that scholastic theology was the only kind of medieval theology began to be questioned between 1940 and 1950 when Etienne Gilson defended Bernard of Clairvaux as a profound dogmatic and mystical theologian, not just a pious preacher. In the same way, McGinn has described a "grassroots theology" in medieval women mystics and those such as Francis whereby the authority to teach came about not *ex officio* but rather *ex beneficio* or by the gift of grace.[16]

Just as monastic theology has been retrieved from the historical closet of piety so too vernacular theology is finding its way into the mainstream of experiential theology. Regis Armstrong indicates that in the Middle Ages theology was to "teach of God, to be taught by God, and to lead to God" (*theologia Deum docet, a Deo docetur, ad Deum ducit*).[17] If theology is essentially "from God to God" then it would be difficult to distil theology from the spiritual journey itself. Zachary Hayes has suggested that a certain kind of logic connects Franciscan spirituality and Franciscan theology through three key themes: the humanity of Christ, the mystery of God as generous love, and the sense of creation as family. Focusing on the development of the Christological theme in the writings of Bonaventure and Scotus, he points to an integral

[12]Alexander Gerken, "The Theological Intuition of St. Francis of Assisi," trans. Ignatius McCormick, *Greyfriars Review*, 7.1 (1993): 71.
[13]Bernard McGinn, *Meister Eckhart and the Beguine Mystics* (New York: Continuum, 1983), 7.
[14]Knox, 175.
[15]McGinn, *Beguine Mystics*, 6.
[16]Bernard McGinn, *The Flowering of Mysticism: Men and Women in the New Mysticism—1200-1350* (New York: Crossroad, 1998), 21.
[17]Regis Armstrong, "Francis of Assisi and the Prisms of Theologizing," *Greyfriars Review*, 10.2 (1994): 179.

connection between the Franciscan intellectual tradition and evangelical life.[18]

Michael Blastic has described early Franciscan life as "doing theology," meaning that, in the beginning of the movement, Franciscan theology was essential to the Franciscan form of life.[19] He draws upon the *Vita prima* of Thomas of Celano to support the link between theology and life, stating that evangelical life is an integrated life of contemplative action, a life which is theological by definition."[20] According to Blastic, Celano developed a Franciscan worldview based on three theological intuitions of Francis: 1) the Christian relation to the world; 2) the meaning of the human Christ, and 3) the nature of the human person.[21] From these three basic points, Celano construed an evangelical form of life in which theology was integrally related to the shape of the life. This symbiotic relationship between theology and *forma vitae* in Celano's writings could be described as a Franciscan evangelical synthesis meaning that Franciscan gospel life is theological by definition.

Although Blastic's argument is persuasive, recent evidence by Timothy Johnson suggests that Celano's synthesis may not have been entirely faithful to Francis's original interpretation of the Gospel but rather an effort to create a literary corpus for an increasingly literate community of brothers.[22] As the number of learned brothers (trained clerics) increased in the community, Johnson states, a textual maturity formed within the community centered on readers, writers, and texts. The development of a learned community centered on written texts eventually forced Francis's theological voice to become marginalized. This transition is evident in Celano's later writings such as the *Legenda ad usum chori* in which there is no reference to Francis's own writings

---

[18]Zachary Hayes, "Christ, Word of God and Exemplar of Humanity," *Cord*, 46 (1996): 6.
[19]Michael Blastic, "It Pleases me that You Should Teach Sacred Theology: Franciscans Doing Theology," *Franciscan Studies*, 55 (1998): 14.
[20]Blastic, 2.
[21]Blastic, 4.
[22]Timothy Johnson, "Lost in Sacred Space: Textual Hermeneutics, Liturgical Worship, and Celano's *Legenda ad usum chori*," p. 12. Paper presented at the 36th International Congress on Medieval Studies, May 3, 2001, Kalamazoo, Michigan. Although Johnson's study highlights the use of sacred space, it provides a useful starting point to understand the birth of the Franciscan intellectual tradition.

and the role of Francis shifts from interpreter of Gospel life to thaumaturgist or wonderworker.[23]

While Johnson's thesis may account for the disappearance of Francis as interpreter of evangelical life and for the rise of a textual intellectual tradition, Francis's theological intuitions are still evident in the writings of Bonaventure. As E. R. Daniel writes: "The pattern that Thomas of Celano constructed was developed and interpreted by Bonaventure. The latter made explicit the interior meaning of this construct which Celano had left implicit.".[24] Scholars have shown that Bonaventure's *Legenda maior* depends on Celano's biographies, but Bonaventure uniquely integrates his ideas into a rich theological synthesis that is marked by Christocentricity. His spiritual writings draw upon the theology of Augustine, Pseudo-Dionysius, and Richard of St. Victor, among others, to support an evangelical theological synthesis. This synthesis is an intellectual (theological/philosophical) system of thought that is both faithful to the theological intuitions of Francis and rigorous in its intellectual structure and method.

Zachary Hayes states that Bonaventure grounded the spirituality of Francis in a metaphysical vision centered on Christ thus providing the larger roadmap of reality.[25] Whereas Celano based his evangelical theology on the insights of Francis, Bonaventure took Francis as the object of theological reflection from which emerged his synthesis of God, humanity, and creation metaphysically grounded in Christ the center.[26] His synthesis is truly intellectual and yet at the same time Franciscan and evangelical. The key to his evangelical theology lies in his theology of the Word in which he grounds all reality, all knowledge, and the human search for God.[27] For Bonaventure, knowledge and love are joined together in Christ in such a way that apart from Christ, knowledge is meaningless. Rather, knowledge of Christ is a relationship in love that becomes visibly expressed in the form of one's life.

[23]Johnson, 9-15.
[24]See E. R. Daniel, *The Franciscan Concept of Mission in the High Middle Ages* (New York: Franciscan Institute, 1975) where Daniel shows how Bonaventure builds on Celano's construct of devotion to Christ and compassionate love. See 48.
[25]Hayes, 12.
[26]See Ilia Delio, *Crucified Love: Bonaventure's Mysticism of the Crucified Christ* (Quincy, IL: Franciscan Press, 1998).
[27]Hayes, 9; cf. also Zachary Hayes, "Christology and Metaphysics in the Thought of Bonaventure," *Journal of Religion* (Supplement, 1978): S91; Ilia Delio, "Bonaventure's Metaphysics of the Good," *Theological Studies*, 60.2 (1999): 228-46.

Bonaventure's evangelical theology, therefore, is a theology of wisdom that finds its deepest meaning in Christ the center.

Reflecting on Bonaventure's theology leads me to suggest that, if we are to identify an authentic Franciscan *intellectual* tradition that is both intellectual and authentically evangelical, it would have to be identified in the writings of Bonaventure. It is here that we find new patterns of relationship grounded in a theological metaphysics that lead to a new vision of and relationship to the world. Yet, if the Franciscan intellectual tradition attains its fullness here, it also terminates here. Bonaventure marks a watershed in the tradition insofar as his evangelical synthesis never really took root in the tradition. In fact he seems to have become something of an obscure figure after his death in 1274.[28] It is interesting that his spiritual writings reemerged in the fifteenth century when the scholastic synthesis was on the point of collapse and modernity began to rise amidst the crisis of western thought. Although Bonaventure has rightly been described as within the Franciscan school, I would suggest that only after him did the Franciscan intellectual tradition take on a more concrete shape as a textual community of learned scholars.[29] By this I mean that there was no continued development of an evangelical synthesis after Bonaventure.[30] Rather, the Franciscan intellectual tradition matured as

---

[28]André Vauchez, "Canonization of St. Thomas and St. Bonaventure: Why a Two-Century Gap Between Them?" trans. Edward Hagman, *Greyfriars Review*, 12.2 (1998): 207 The earliest account of Bonaventure's life dates from the time of his canonization in 1482. Whatever delayed the recognition of Bonaventure's holiness, it seems to have faded with time. By the fifteenth century, Bonaventure's works became influential, particularly because the great theological syntheses were in crisis and mystical tendencies were on the rise. In a letter of 1426, for example, Jean Gerson was deeply shocked that the Franciscan Order had not shown more zeal in promoting the canonization of Bonaventure whom he considered the most reliable and commendable theologian. The Council of Florence in 1440 also reintroduced the works of Bonaventure in view of negotiations with the Byzantine Church; George Marcil, "The Franciscan School through the Centuries," in *The History of Franciscan Theology*, ed. Kenan Osborne (New York: The Franciscan Institute, 1994), 319-20. Marcil also notes Bonanventure's revival in the fifteenth century and indicates that a Jesuit by the name of Peter Trigoso de Calatayud, who later switched to the Capuchin Order, published in 1593 a Bonaventurian study of theology that to some degree likened Bonaventure to Thomas Aquinas.

[29]By "textual community" I mean a community centered on the interpretation of written texts rather than on lived experience. Brian Stock describes textual communities as "microsocieties organized around the common understanding of a script." Community members employ texts for literary and social purposes which in turn influence the historical context and consequences of their actions. See Brian Stock, *Listening for the Text: On the Uses of the Past* (Philadelphia: University of Pennsylvania Press, 1997), 22-23; Johnson, "Lost in Sacred Space," 3.

[30]I would like to note that women did not achieve a level of authority in the development of the tradition, at least from an historical perspective. The lack of women's

a literary community that gradually moved away from theological reflection on Francis's life to an emphasis on the interpretation of texts. Thus, the tradition retreated from the context of evangelical life, especially as it encountered changing cultural conditions.

The Franciscan School

In his essay on "The Franciscan School through the Centuries," the late George Marcil wrote: "One sees with difficulty a well-defined school arising from the Assisi experience [of Francis]. It is not easy to conceive an intellectual system wrought out of a set of ideas when love and free will are at the center of the package."[31] Implicit in Marcil's statement is the idea that the whole notion of an intellectual tradition is rather tenuous when held up to the free spirit of Francis of Assisi. In light of this, or rather because of this idea, he identifies the Franciscan intellectual tradition as a school rather than as a tradition related to the life. He asserts that Anthony of Padua marks the beginning of the school, which progresses through the three great intellectual pillars—Bonaventure, Scotus, Ockham, and their disciples—and on into the time of the renaissance, reformation, post-reformation, and twentieth century. The notion of a school further indicates that the Franciscan intellectual tradition developed within the academy and within a textual community and not necessarily in the context of lived experience.

If we speculate that the Franciscan intellectual tradition as evangelical *tradition* never really progressed beyond the thirteenth century, then we must ask, who are the real witnesses to this tradition? Are they the great theologians and philosophers of the Franciscan Order? Are they the friars and sisters in the soup kitchens? Or are they the scholars with doctorates in medieval theology? It seems to me that what transpired, although unintentionally, was the conflation of the Franciscan intellectual tradition and the Franciscan school in such a way

---

voices in the growth of the intellectual tradition supports the collapse of the evangelical synthesis and the rise of a learned intellectual tradition that presupposed a university education, a privilege denied to women.

[31]Marcil, 311. Although Marcil argues in favor of a Franciscan school, he does imply that the tradition itself belies a "school mentality" when he writes: "There is something in the Franciscan spirit that calls for freedom. That spirit seems to be opposed to a "school" mentality. It is one thing to have a general direction for one's meditation and study; it is quite another to have a strictly regimented intellectual program."

that the Franciscan school developed as a tradition within a tradition, governed by its own ethos, identity, and set of values. The bearers of the tradition became an elite corps of educated friars that hardly represented an Order that had grown in a variety of ways.[32] As an intellectual *school* it gave primacy to texts and remained faithful to the scholastic synthesis, perhaps clinging to it more tenaciously as the tradition encountered the crisis of modernity. Apart from this, however, the intellectual tradition remained apathetic to the changing context of the life itself.

This leads me to conclude that what we call today the Franciscan intellectual tradition is not really a tradition that informs Franciscan life but a school of thought that has attracted the educated. It is not surprising, therefore, that only a few Franciscans know anything about the Franciscan intellectual tradition. When Franciscan seminarians are questioned about studying theology, for example, some will say: "I am not interested in studying theology because I want to do ministry." As if studying theology is an impediment to ministry or ministry is something that one does apart from theology. Those who pursue the Master of Divinity degree usually obtain a solid foundation in Karl Rahner's theology and complete their theological studies with barely a thought about Bonaventure or Scotus's theology other than what might have filtered through Rahner. Even more surprising are those who study Bonaventure and remark: "Bonaventure is just like Rahner!" I don't think it is an exaggeration to state that contemporary Franciscan life has become shapeless because our theology has become eclectic, the result of a fragmented evangelical synthesis of theology and lived experience.

If Franciscan evangelical life has been detached from its theological/philosophical underpinnings, the split has been furthered by the entrenched Thomism that has governed Roman Catholicism since the nineteenth century. Marcil says that Scotus became to Franciscans

---

[32]The word "Order" here is used in the widest sense to include the whole Franciscan family, that is, First Order (friars), Second Order (Poor Clares), and Third Order (religious and secular). I would also include Franciscan secular institutes. Giovanni Immarone points out that the First Order can be subdivided into the three separate branches, that is, Observant, Conventual, and Capuchin, each with their own autonomous way of life, traditions, values, and legislation. See Giovanni Immarone, "Franciscan Theology Today: Its Possibility, Necessity and Value," trans. Lori Pieper, *Greyfriars Review*, 8.1 (1994): 103-26.

what Thomas was to Dominicans;[33] yet, Scotus's theology never became a household product compared to that of Thomas Aquinas. Thomism was given ecclesiastical support through the encyclical *Aeterni Patris* [1879], which mandated the teaching of Thomas's theology in all seminaries, Catholic colleges and universities. For the Franciscan intellectual tradition, Thomistic theology provided a theological wedge that furthered the split between theology and lived experience. By the early twentieth century, Franciscan life wound up on a tripod: theology belonged to Thomas, the charism belonged to Francis, and the form of life belonged to Benedict (a monastic structure of life that Francis himself renounced).[34] What originated with Francis and Clare, therefore—the synthesis of thought and feeling, content and form, theory and practice expressed in the integration of God, humanity, and cosmos—was not only lost but shattered as the intellectual tradition consolidated into a school. We are only now beginning to pick up the pieces.

Contemporary Concerns

The idea that the Franciscan intellectual tradition has had little or no influence on the contemporary form of Franciscan life became evident at the annual gathering of the provincials of the English Speaking Conference of the Friars Minor (ESC-OFM) last year in Colorado Springs. Basic questions concerning the tradition were brought to their attention in discussions of the future of the Order. These questions centered around three basic points: What is the Franciscan intellectual tradition? How does it relate to Franciscan life? What is its future? In a sense, the questions were startling because they indicated to the provincials that both the meaning and purpose of the Franciscan intellectual tradition were essentially unknown. As a result, a task force on the Franciscan intellectual tradition was established to try to address these concerns. Joseph Chinnici, O.F.M., assisted by Margaret Carney, O.S.F., and Edward Coughlin, O.F.M., organized the task force with the following goals: 1) identification of the intellectual

---

[33]Marcil, 317.
[34]According to the *Speculum perfectionis*, Francis did not want to be bothered with the Rules of St. Benedict or Augustine. See *Francis of Assisi: Early Documents*, vol. 3, *The Prophet*, ed. Regis J. Armstrong, J. A. Wayne Hellmann, and William Short (New York: New City Press, 2001), 314.

tradition per se; 2) assessment of initial and ongoing formation within the tradition; 3) collaboration between the various Franciscan study centers; 4) examination of the means and promotion of publications; 5) mobilization of resources for globalization. While the work of the task force is still ongoing (now an established committee under the aegis of the ESC-OFM), I would like to note the work of Joseph Chinnici who has been a key figure in the renewal of contemporary evangelical life.

Over the last several years, Chinnici has raised a significant voice concerning the integral relationship between the Franciscan intellectual tradition and Franciscan evangelical life. In a paper entitled, "North American Stewardship of the Franciscan Intellectual Tradition," he pointed to a "copernican shift"[35] in Franciscan identity with the publication of the critical edition of the writings of Francis by Cajetan Esser in 1976. Since that time, Chinnici writes, "the Franciscan family in the United States has taken a major step in articulating the distinctiveness of the Franciscan charism in its evangelical dimension."[36] He further points out that soon after Esser's work and that of Ignatius Brady, European scholarship on Franciscan identity and life began to flourish, especially among lay scholars. Over the last decade, a series of critical studies in Europe have appeared which highlight the place of the Franciscan family and its origins within the context of western European culture and society. Jacques LeGoff, for example, has argued for the relationship between Franciscan life and a social mutation in western thinking and structures. Ovidio Capitani has described Francis as a paradigm of a "new anthropology," one which is "willing in the conversion to poverty to engage the changing face of society, and from within the struggles of society to preach the Gospel."[37] Based on this new scholarship, Chinnici writes: "What the Franciscan intellectual tradition argued for in its time was a different type of presence in society, a different type of relationship with God and the world than that defined by the inherited 'thought style' of the Gregorian reform."[38]

The significance of the new European scholarship, Chinnici indicates, is its focus on the impact of the early Franciscan tradition. The rise of the tradition in the thirteenth century had a significant

---

[35]Joseph P. Chinnici, "North American Stewardship of the Franciscan Intellectual Tradition," 5. Paper presented at the Franciscan Institute, July 11, 2000.
[36]Chinnici, 5.
[37]Chinnici, 6-7.
[38]Chinnici, 7.

influence on Church and society, and this influence, emerging out of the theological experiences of Francis and Clare, manifested itself on the levels of politics, society, economics, and culture. In light of this scholarship, Chinnici points to the *kairos* of the present moment as a two-edged sword. While new translations and commentaries on early Franciscan writings, coupled with the new European scholarship, are disclosing the primitive evangelical synthesis, we are, at the same time, losing the personal and social carriers of the tradition's wisdom. "As a result," he writes:

> The presentation and handing on of the intellectual patrimony has been generally de-institutionalized and placed on the shoulders of individual scholars precisely at that point when a new public presence in Church and society is most demanded and needed. The individuals themselves feel a loss of this institutional support, and the mantle of scholarly reflection on the Franciscan life and from within it is quickly passing to a generation of people who do not have the same lived experience. Theology is being driven from its social and experiential base in the family itself. This will necessarily affect the interpretation of our life in the years to come.[39]

Although Chinnici does not distinguish between the Franciscan intellectual school and the tradition itself, what he brings to light is that, for the first time in centuries, we have the capacity to renew the tradition and to restore the evangelical synthesis of theology and lived experience. At the same time, however, the problems facing this work of renewal are enormous. In his report to the provincials this year, Chinnici summed up the principal concerns regarding the intellectual tradition today:

1) the consolidation, closure, and institutional loss of programs of learning.
2) The loss of control over theological curriculum and the acceptance of an eclectic intellectual tradition.
3) The reliance on small centers, isolated one from the other, with overworked people to carry the freight of the entire family.

---

[39]Chinnici, 8.

4) The appeal by different places for economic and personnel resources from the same supplying bodies, which themselves are torn in other directions.
5) The competition between study centers for teachers, administrators, publications, visibility, and students.
6) The attempt to mainstream a Franciscan vision, with difficulty, in colleges and universities.
7) The declining number of scholars capable of working with the original text, that is, the loss of language training.[40]

These points basically sum up the comment made by the German scholar, J. Lang, who, in a 1975 article on Franciscan theology, pointed to the "miserable" state of "sterility" in Franciscan theology.[41] Lang attributed this sterility, in part, to the indifference of the Franciscan Order to studies. Lang's point, while *prima facie* a negative one, underlies the historical tension within the Order between (formal) study and ministry. Study belongs to the training of clerics and scholars while ministry refers to the apostolate of the friars. These two dimensions have little in common with one another because without a proper understanding of evangelical life there is no common ground.

An Optimistic Future?

We find ourselves today at a crossroads of new life and slow death. We are just beginning to discover the richness of the Franciscan intellectual tradition. The texts and tools to establish new life are at hand, and yet, the opportunities to promote scholarship and new scholars are diminishing. The Franciscan tradition finds itself on shifting sands as it seeks to revitalize and integrate the intellectual tradition into its way of life. If the intellectual tradition is intended to be at the heart of the life itself, and the resources to sustain this intellectual tradition are diminishing, what does this say about the life? Certainly, without appropriate content, the life itself lacks form; and without form, it lacks meaning and is reduced to a privatized spirituality. As the Franciscan intellectual tradition faces a diminishing future, therefore,

---

[40]Joseph P. Chinnici, "Report of the Task Force on the Franciscan Intellectual Tradition to the ESC-OFM Conference," Colorado Springs, 2001, p. 5.
[41]J. Lang, "Gibt es heute eine franziskanische Theologie?" *Franziskanische Studien*, 57 (1975): 37-45.

Franciscan life becomes ever more an interesting but purely private option. As a privatized spirituality, it can offer nothing to a world crying out for justice and peace.

We need to reclaim the Franciscan intellectual tradition from the throes of privatization (and from the school mentality) both as an influential power to shape Franciscan life and as a public theological voice in a pluralistic world. While there are a number of fine scholars outside the tradition who are making substantial contributions to the intellectual tradition per se, the real thrust of contemporary Franciscan theology must come from within the group. This is not to presume an elitist position but simply to highlight the fact that Franciscan theology is a reflective theology and as such, one that takes as its source of reflection the Christian experience of Francis and Clare. That is, the intellectual tradition forms the architectonics of the life itself so that the intellectual tradition and *forma vitae* comprise the distinct charism we call Franciscan evangelical life.

Chinnici has argued for a "domestication" of the tradition, that is, making the theological/philosophical tradition accessible and understandable to the Franciscan family around the (English- speaking) world. The purpose of the committee on the renewal of the Franciscan intellectual tradition will be to promote this "domestication."

Collaboration between study centers, publishing houses, ongoing formation groups, and other efforts will be explored to enhance the tradition. While new relationships of collaboration will help to revitalize the tradition, something more basic is needed at the heart of the life itself. I suggest that what we need is something like *conversio morum suorum*,[42] that is, a process of acquiring new attitudes and behaviors that in turn can be expressed in new patterns of relationships. We need a process integrated into Franciscan life to develop a theological *habitus* (or what Alexander of Hales called a *habitus fidei*). Maybe it is time to encourage Franciscan communities to become communities of theological reflection, incorporating core theological

---

[42]The term "conversio morum suorum," as Benedictine scholars point out, is a difficult one to define precisely. According to the *Dictionnaire de Spiritualité*, it means a "conversion of one's behavior, the abandonment of secular habits and adherence to monastic practice," that is, the total conversion of the individual to a solitary (*monachos*) way of life. The same idea is applied here to a Franciscan way of life not as a solitary one but rather as evangelical. See *Dictionnaire de Spiritualité*, 2:2206-2212.

values into their way of life by a process of reflection that will inform new structures of consciousness.

A way of life that is shaped by Franciscan theology and philosophy will ultimately make a difference in Church and society if it is articulated by a corporate voice. Theological reflection, therefore, must take place on every level of Franciscan life, within first, second, and third order communities, secular institutes and secular Franciscan life. We may not all speak the same dialect but what grasps us in the core of our identity should be similar. Basic attitudes such as the goodness of God, the primacy of Christ, and the dignity of the human person must comprise the basis of our worldview.

Tradition is about dialogue, speaking the past in the present with one another and with the world, so that what is most valuable and authentic may continue to grow precisely in the form of identity. Religious tradition emerges within a faith community, and only from the community can a theological voice be in dialogue with the world and offer the world a new experience of God. The Franciscan tradition is no exception. In this respect, everyone, including lay scholars working within the tradition, must be given a place in the Franciscan family in which they may speak, be heard, and participate in the unfolding of the evangelical theological vision, especially if it is to have a meaningful public voice.

What we need to keep in mind is that the Franciscan intellectual tradition is not meant to rest on intellectual elitism but on the ultimate goodness of God. At the heart of this tradition is the Incarnation, which signifies to us that the search for true knowledge can never be an abstract pursuit. Rather knowledge is meaningful when it is embodied in human persons and expressed in the form of love. The Franciscan intellectual tradition, therefore, cannot be confined to texts but rather must be placed in the context of life. It is a tradition that finds its deepest meaning in the human person and in relationship to the world. In short we might say that the tradition is intended to be a public tradition because it has, at its center, transformation of the world in Christ. Knowledge, therefore, must be informed by love and expressed in action for knowledge is not an end in itself but a path to God.

Conclusion

The French scholar Anton Péguy has described the reform of tradition as *ressourcement*, implying a return to the origin by way of advance "from a less perfect tradition to one more perfect; from a shallower tradition to one more profound; by withdrawal of tradition to a new depth."[43] We are at a period of *ressourcement* in the Franciscan tradition, a time of renewal, or perhaps of discovery, as we come to a more authentic understanding of the Franciscan intellectual tradition. We cannot return to the thirteenth century but we can retrieve something of its essential meaning in the twenty-first century. What we hope for is a new depth in the tradition, one that enables us to move forward with a new level of understanding.

While we recognize the importance of the Franciscan intellectual tradition in relationship to Franciscan life, the experience of the present moment seems more chaotic than hopeful. The old order is dissipating and the emergence of something new is yet unknown. Delwin Brown says that the dynamism of any tradition lies precisely in the dialectic between chaos and order.[44] This idea should signal to us that the Franciscan intellectual tradition is dynamic and alive despite the chaos and uncertainty of the present. Perhaps we can learn to navigate through this labyrinth of uncertainty by learning from the new science. The science of chaos, for example, tells us that new patterns of order emerge in dissipating systems only when systems are open to new influences. Is the Franciscan intellectual tradition a system open to new influences? Can it be changed by new structures of relationship, by new patterns of thinking? Even more importantly, can it function as a *system*, that is, in cooperative relationships among its members?

Margaret Wheatley tells us that a system grows and develops as a whole or not at all. This is a lesson for us who still function in many ways like parts of a Newtonian universe. We are autonomous individual communities, scholars, colleges, study centers, etc., each with our own self-enclosed structures, wary of collaboration unless it has some type of remuneration. Yet, as Wheatley indicates, in a system each part is something of the whole and parts must function together if meaning is

---

[43]Cited in Congar, "The Meaning of Tradition," 12.
[44]Brown, *Boundaries of Our Habitation*, 87.

to be generated by a coherent vision and pattern of values.[45] Our purpose is to explore the Franciscan intellectual tradition by asking how we can generate a coherent vision and pattern of values that give direction and meaning to this tradition. Can we work together to create a public voice in the Church and world that is a distinctly Franciscan voice? Wheatley provides insight to these questions when she writes:

> In this new world, you and I make it up as we go along, not because we lack expertise or planning skills, but because that is the nature of reality. Reality changes shape and meaning because of our activity. And it is constantly new. We are required to be there, as active participants. It can't happen without us and nobody can do it for us.[46]

And herein is our hope—the meaning of the Franciscan intellectual tradition is ours to name and ours to change. It is we who are the bearers and witnesses of this tradition. We are to begin to live it anew, therefore, because the tradition has no meaning without us and no one will create it for us.

---

[45]Margaret J. Wheatley, *Leadership and the New Science: Learning about Organization from an Orderly Universe* (San Francisco: Berrett-Koehler Publishers Inc., 1994), 127.
[46]Wheatley, 151.

Chapter Two

FRANCIS AS VERNACULAR THEOLOGIAN: A LINK TO THE FRANCISCAN INTELLECTUAL TRADITION?[1]

Dominic Monti, O.F.M.

If we were holding a symposium on the Franciscan Intellectual Tradition fifty years ago, a paper with this title would have seemed very much out of place. To some it still might. After all, what has the Poverello in common with Bonaventure or Scotus—other than being a brother? For the past number of years now the Franciscan Institute of St. Bonaventure University has recognized men and women who have made outstanding contributions to Franciscan scholarship. The handsome medal conferred to the recipient on that occasion has the busts of four figures: Anthony of Padua, Bonaventure, John Duns Scotus, and William of Ockham. All of them were teachers; three were men of acknowledged sanctity, two of whom have been officially proclaimed as Doctors of the Church. The fourth was a brilliant theologian, although a condemned heretic.[2] However, the figure of Francis is missing from the group. But isn't this as it should be? Isn't Francis simply in another league? A great saint undoubtedly, but a shaper of an intellectual tradition? It would not seem so at first glance.

First of all, Francis would hardly have considered himself within this context. In his *Letter to the Entire Order*, he describes himself in a famous phrase as *simplex et idiota*: "an ignorant, uneducated person."[3]

---

[1]While I was putting the last touches on the written text of this presentation on September 11, 2001, my work was interrupted by news of the terrorist attacks on the United States. Later that day, I learned that one of the New York victims of that tragedy was Mychal Judge, O.F.M., a friar of my province. I dedicate this article to his memory. Mychal showed himself a true brother to everyone he met, bringing God's message of love to them in the vernacular of our times.
[2]Perhaps this medal captures the Franciscan intellectual tradition as a whole: one officially acknowledged by the Church, but always potentially threatening to its current institutional structures.
[3]LtOrd, 39. For the meaning of these terms, see Octavian Schmucki, "St. Francis's Level of Education," *Greyfriars Review* 10 (1996): 153-171. The translation of this phrase in *Francis and Clare: The Complete Works*, ed. R. Armstrong and I. Brady (New York:

Now it is important to recognize that Francis is clearly exaggerating here. He was considerably more educated than the vast majority of his contemporaries by the simple fact that he could read and write.[4] But by the time Francis composed this letter near the end of his life, he was profoundly conscious of the fact that a growing number of his brothers possessed a level of formal theological education that he did not. The *simplex et idiota* phrase occurs in a section of the letter dealing with liturgical matters, so Francis is making clear that he is not writing as an expert. Rather, he confesses his dependence "on the priests of the Order."[5] We know too that he expressed gratefulness to those who possessed such expertise: "We must honor all theologians and those who minister the most holy divine words and respect them as those who minister to us spirit and life."[6] But it is clear that Francis did not count himself among such theologians. His own words, then, seem to remove him from being considered in program on the Franciscan Intellectual Tradition.

Furthermore, at least some thirteenth-century sources portray Francis as being very uncomfortable with, if not actually hostile to, his brothers' increasing attraction to learning. In a collection of stories, most likely related by Brother Leo in the 1250s, Francis not only advises a provincial minister to give up his personal library, but repeatedly resists the request of a novice to be allowed his own Psalter.[7] As Leo summarizes:

> Blessed Francis did not want his brothers to be desirous of learning and books, but wanted and preached to the brothers to be eager to have and to imitate pure and holy simplicity, holy prayer, and Lady Poverty, on which [foundations] the holy and first brothers had built.

Paulist Press, 1982), 59) is more accurate than that in *Francis of Assisi: Early Documents*, Vol. 1, ed. R. Armstrong, W. Hellmann and W. Short (Hyde Park, NY: New City Press, 1999-2001), 119. The latter publication will hereafter be referred to as *FA: ED*, followed by volume and page number.

[4]Schmucki concludes: "Because of his formal education, limited though it was, he stood halfway between the 'unlettered' or 'simple' and the 'literate' or 'learned' members of his Order," 170.

[5]LtOrd, 38 (*FA: ED*, 1: 119).

[6]Test, 13 (*FA: ED*, 1: 125).

[7]AC 102-105 (*FA: ED*, 2: 206-210). For the dating of this material, cf. AC, 115-116.

Now Leo certainly had to admit that Francis did not "despise or disdain holy knowledge."[8] But he did appear to be apprehensive about the pride and self-satisfaction that learning often engendered, the possessions that formal study would require, and, above all, the seeming incompatibility of scholarship with the "spirit of prayer and devotion."[9] For Francis, a focus on mastering the letter of the divine text could all too easily quench the Spirit.[10]

It was for both of these reasons—that Francis himself was not highly educated and his ambivalent attitude towards academic pursuits among his brothers—that historians of the Franciscan intellectual tradition have not directly incorporated the Order's founder as part of that history. For example, Philotheus Boehner's classic *History of the Franciscan School* described it as "the work of Franciscan [thinkers], who lived in a Franciscan atmosphere, and were formed by the Franciscan way of life" and thus "were animated by a Franciscan spirit." Boehner does not present Francis himself as directly contributing to the work of the school bearing his name: he enters the story as the person who sparked the birth of the Franciscan movement by his desire to realize the Gospel ideal in a radical way. In this way, Francis and his first companions created "the atmosphere" and laid the foundations for the "way of life" that nurtured and animated the "Franciscan spirit" characterizing those of his brothers who did make intellectual contributions.[11]

Boehner's view is reflected in the recent *History of Franciscan Theology*, a team effort by a number of prominent scholars. Like Boehner, they focus their attention on the century that begins with the Franciscan school of theology at Paris in the 1230s and ends with the doctrinal disputes that wracked the Order in the 1320s and 30s. But this history begins after Francis's death. He does not directly enter the story.[12] Neither do others. In the closing chapter of this volume,

---

[8]AC 103 (2: 207).
[9]This is precisely the *caveat* Francis expressed when he gave his permission for Anthony to teach the brothers in Bologna (*FA: ED*, 1: 107).
[10]Cf. Adm 7 (*FA: ED*, 1: 132).
[11]Philotheus Boehner, *The History of the Franciscan School*, Vol. 1 (Detroit: Duns Scotus College, 1947), 4-9.
[12]The editor of this volume, Kenan Osborne, does include Francis in a more explicit way than did Boehner, however: "What we today name as Franciscan theology or a Franciscan school was created by a process involving many writers.   . . . Francis of Assisi of course stands at the foundation of this process, even though his writings cannot be called in any technical sense a 'theology.' . . . [His] vision of the gospel way of life,

Margaret Carney addresses the contributions of women to the Franciscan theological enterprise. She admits from the outset that this is difficult to assess due to the simple fact that women could not formally participate in that enterprise during this creative period. They "were excluded from the universities and from the clerical ministries which would have placed them among professional theologians." However, she goes on to suggest that "if we think of that branch of theology which devotes itself to the study of spiritual experience, . . . we may find a path by which to trace the impact of Franciscan women upon its development." Here Carney alludes to the fact that modern scholars have been re-thinking the whole concept of theology as understood in the Middle Ages by exploring, for example, the symbiotic relation that existed at that time between academic theology and spiritual pedagogy. Such a broadening of the discussion would also include the contributions of Franciscan women such as Clare of Assisi and Angela of Foligno. "By sharing their experience of God" they may well have had a profound "impact upon the resources from which scholars derive their intellectual constructs."[13]

I believe that this turn in scholarship to which Carney refers also opens a path by which Francis himself might be incorporated into the Franciscan intellectual tradition. Carney makes the point about widening the concept of "theologian" in order to include women within that tradition. However, the more fundamental issue is not simply the inclusion of women—an important task to be sure!—but the inclusion of non-academics, a larger group to which all medieval women belonged. In other words, if we are able to broaden our understanding of theology, admitting the validity of a new category—"vernacular theology"—it might allow a *simplex et idiota* like Francis to be included among our theologians after all.[14]

---

however, found an echo in the process which developed into a technical theology." *The History of Franciscan Theology*, ed. Kenan Osborne (St. Bonaventure, NY: The Franciscan Institute, 1994), 16. Osborne recognizes here that Francis's writings might indeed contain a theology, although not in the technical sense that I describe in subsequent paragraphs.

[13] *The History of Franciscan Theology*, 336-337.

[14] When my colleague, Ilia Delio, and I were planning this symposium, we had originally invited Dr. Bernard McGinn to give this presentation, as he has been in the forefront of those who are proposing the new concept of "vernacular theology." When he was unable to do so, I consented, but confessed that my own insights on this topic would be highly dependent on his work, a fact that will be evident from the references which follow. McGinn's significant contribution to Franciscan scholarship, culminating with the extensive treatment of Franciscan spirituality in his work, *The Flowering of Mysticism: Men*

Just who is a theologian? If we search a basic reference work, we will find a definition something like the following: "Theologian, professional practitioner of theology, which is the scientific study of God and of God's relationship to the world."[15] Given such a definition, it is understandable that such "professional practitioners"—Bonaventure, John Duns Scotus and William of Ockham—would dominate any history of the Franciscan theological tradition. But we must also understand that our modern definition of "theology" has been very much influenced by developments particular to Western culture. Today, the word "theology" connotes both the "scientific study" of God and a "professional practitioner." But it is important to realize that such was not always the case.

These qualifying phrases came to describe theology in the wake of the great intellectual movement we call Scholasticism. This movement, which was less than one hundred years old when Francis was born, actually represented a novel approach to understanding God and God's relation to the world. In one respect it was simply another manifestation of the drive for order that characterized twelfth-century society in general. The Scholastics embarked on a "scientific study" of the Christian faith, characterized by three techniques: a methodical commentary on authoritative texts, the systematic analysis and solution of dogmatic and moral issues arising from those texts, and the synthetic effort to draw together a coherent and comprehensive presentation of Christian doctrine for instructional purposes.[16] Such a sophisticated method demanded "professional practitioners," who created a special institution (the university) and adopted a style of life designed to facilitate the full-time pursuit of their specialized tasks. As is evident from our present-day definition, these innovations permanently transformed the Western understanding of theology. But we should recognize that our modern preconceptions also determined the way in

---

and Women in the New Mysticism (New York: Crossroad, 1998), was acknowledged when the Franciscan Institute chose him as the recipient of its medal that year.

[15]*HarperCollins Encyclopedia of Catholicism*, ed. Richard McBrien (HarperSanFrancisco, 1995), 1249. This brief entry is unsigned, but I suspect that it was composed by the eminent author of the accompanying entry "theology," Gerard O'Collins.

[16]For example, Bonaventure, a Scholastic theologian, contributed works in all three categories: 1) Biblical commentaries, 2) a *Commentary on the Sentences of Peter Lombard* and several series of "Disputed Questions," and 3) the *Breviloquium*. My description of the scholastic method draws on Bernard McGinn, *The Growth of Mysticism*, Vol. 2 of *The Presence of God: A History of Western Christian Mysticism* (New York: Crossroad, 1994), 367-374.

which historians have treated medieval theology. For a long time, we were under the impression that the only form of theology being practiced in the Middle Ages was the Scholastic one. For Catholics, this tendency was reinforced by the neo-Scholastic movement of the century between 1860 and 1960, when Church leaders were emphasizing that this highly technical expression of faith was normative for all time.

Part of the intellectual renewal movement within the Catholic Church that lead up to the Second Vatican Council was a renewal of Biblical, patristic, and medieval studies, which drew attention to the fact that there were other valid forms of the "understanding of faith" that did not employ Scholastic methods and categories. It was only at this time that scholars began to recognize that another type of theology was flourishing in the Middle Ages. Actually, it was one of the great neo-Scholastic thinkers, Etienne Gilson, who pioneered this effort in the 1930s when he broke open the profound dogmatic theology of Bernard of Clairvaux, a figure viewed up to that time as "merely" a great preacher and mystical writer. But it was not until the 1950s that Jean Leclercq began developing the concept of a "monastic theology" that was different in method and setting from Scholasticism, but no less important in expressing and shaping medieval Christians' understanding of faith. Historians came to recognize just how much monastic thinkers, who were not in any way professional academicians and did not necessarily express themselves in scientific terminology, were cited as theological authorities by Scholastic authors themselves.[17]

Now, over the past two decades, a new wave of scholars, many of them in the emerging field of spirituality, have sought to broaden the traditional categories even further. Did not many mystical writers who were neither professional academics nor cloistered religious express insights about the nature of God and God's relationship to the world that were also insightful? In other words, can we not learn profound things about God from a lay woman like Julian of Norwich as well as from a Scholastic theologian like Thomas Aquinas?

The Church itself—often notoriously slow—seems to be moving in this direction. Since 1970, three women have been declared Doctors of

---

[17]See Bernard McGinn, *Meister Eckhart and the Beguine Mystics* (New York: Continuum, 1994), 4-6. Leclercq summarizes the relation between monastic and scholastic theology in "The Renewal of Theology," *Renaissance and Renewal in the Twelfth Century*, ed. Robert Benson and Giles Constable (Cambridge: Harvard University Press, 1982), 68-87.

the Church. All were non-ordained Christians who were neither professionally trained nor formally recognized as teachers in their own day. John Paul II's proclamation in 1997 of Thérèse of Lisieux as an official "teacher" of the things of God is especially striking. As a woman who had no formal education beyond the eighth grade and died at the age of twenty-four, she was certainly no "professional practitioner" of theology. And her "Little Way" does not employ traditional theological categories and the usual "scientific" form of theological analysis. Yet the deep spiritual wisdom she expresses in everyday language has exercised a major influence over the past century, not just on the level of popular piety, but on major Christian intellectuals as well.[18]

By the way, just to illustrate how quickly ideas can change, I draw attention to the article in the *New Catholic Encyclopedia* on "Doctor of the Church," written just three years before the elevation of Teresa of Avila and Catherine of Siena to that category. It stated: "It would seem that no woman is likely to be named [doctor] because of the link between this title and the teaching office, which is limited to males."[19] On the contrary, it would seem that recent Popes have not agreed with the author's assumption that the teaching office is limited to professional academics or members of the hierarchy. Rather, ordinary people, non-specialists—the *simplices et idiotae*—can also be recognized as individuals who have formulated a profound teaching about God. After all, is not the whole enterprise of Christian theology founded upon the challenging insights about God proposed by an uneducated Jewish carpenter venerated as a Rabbi by his disciples?

The growing recognition of the contributions of many non-professional theologians to the task of deepening the understanding of Christian faith has led Bernard McGinn, a leading specialist in medieval thought, to coin a new term—"vernacular theology"—to characterize their work.[20] The word "vernacular" is a happy choice, because it captures the chief characteristic of this third mode of medieval religious thought as distinguished from both "Scholastic theology" and "monastic

---

[18]Again, I am dependent on a work of Bernard McGinn, *The Doctors of the Church: Twenty-Three Men and Women Who Shaped Christianity* (New York: Crossroad, 1999), 1-21. On Thérèse, see 169-173.

[19]*New Catholic Encyclopedia*, 4: 939. I owe this reference to McGinn, *Doctors*, xii.

[20]McGinn first introduced this concept in *Meister Eckhart and the Beguine Mystics* (1994), 4-14, and has further developed it in *The Flowering of Mysticism*, which is Vol. 3 of his monumental *The Presence of God: A History of Western Mysticism* (1998), especially 18-24.

theology," namely, its linguistic expression in the burgeoning vernacular languages of medieval Europe. As the present controversy within the Church over the appropriate translation of Latin liturgical texts has made abundantly clear, language gives rise to thought. The two recognized types of medieval theology—Scholastic and monastic—were expressed in Latin. McGinn points out that Latin in the Middle Ages possessed certain advantages—"its weight of sacrality, its Scholastic precision, and its cultural universality." However, he goes on,

> [it] suffered from important disadvantages as well. Latin was at best half-alive in the Middle Ages—never the language of first acquisition, always bound to a male-dominated cultural elite, and regulated by inherited models of linguistic propriety that made innovation difficult. . . . The vernacular languages on the other hand, offered remarkable potential for creative innovation.[21]

A layperson was free to employ bold new forms of conceptualizing God and communicating the religious experience that simply would not occur to most professional theologians. The term "vernacular" also alludes to the fact that this type of theology was directed at an audience very different from the educated elite in the schools of theology or the monks and nuns in their cloisters. It was their desire to communicate to ordinary men and women in the streets that led its practitioners to express their ideas in the vernacular tongues in the first place. As such, they manifest what McGinn has called a process of "democratization and secularization" of religious experience evident in the early thirteenth century. Men and women did not have to become professional "religious" who "fled the world" in order to experience God. Rather, vernacular theologians expressed the conviction that it was indeed possible for *all* Christians to find God *in the midst of* the world.[22]

It is this new concept of vernacular theology that permits us to think of Francis, not simply as a religious genius who sparked an

---

[21]McGinn, *Flowering*, 21. A good illustration of this is the work of the German Franciscan David of Augsburg (+1272), an educated cleric who was also a popular preacher and spiritual director. His Latin treatises, directed to an "in-house" clerical audience, draw largely on the concepts of earlier authors; his thought in them is quite "pedestrian." It is precisely in his vernacular writings that he "experimented with creating new terminology for trinitarian speculation" (McGinn, *Flowering*, 113-116).

[22]McGinn, *Flowering*, 13.

evangelical renewal movement that would come to include great thinkers, but also as one who himself forged new understandings of God and of God's relation to the world. Indeed, McGinn suggests that in light of recent scholarship, "Francis may well be thought of as one of the first major vernacular theologians."[23] Here perhaps we are finally beginning to notice a dimension of Francis that was acknowledged by his own contemporaries. At least two of the early biographical sources portray Francis as a theologian, one who communicated distinctively powerful insights about God and God's relation with us. As related in the *Assisi Compilation,*

> While he was staying in Siena, someone from the Order of Preachers happened to arrive; he was a spiritual man and a Doctor of Sacred Theology. He visited blessed Francis, and he and the holy man enjoyed a long and sweet conversation about the words of the Lord.
>
> This teacher asked him about the words of Ezechiel: *If you do not warn the wicked man about his wickedness, I will hold you responsible for his soul.* "I'm acquainted with many people, good father, who live in mortal sin, as I'm aware. But I don't always warn them about their wickedness. Will I than be held responsible for their souls?"
>
> Blessed Francis then said that he was an unlettered man, and it would be better for him to be taught by the other rather than to answer a question about Scripture. But that humble teacher replied: "Brother, it's true that I have heard these words explained by some wise men; still I'd be glad to hear how you understand it." So blessed Francis said to him: "If that passage is supposed to be understood in a universal sense, then I understand it to mean that a servant of God should be burning with life and holiness so brightly, that by the light of example and the tongue of his conduct, he will rebuke all the wicked. In that way, I say, the brightness of his life and the fragrance of his reputation will *proclaim their wickedness* to all of them."
>
> That man went away greatly edified, and said to the companions of blessed Francis: "My brothers, the theology of this man, held aloft by purity and contemplation, is a *soaring eagle,* while our learning *crawls on its belly on the ground.*"[24]

---

[23]McGinn, *Flowering,* 51-59.
[24]AC 35-36 (*FA: ED,* 2: 140-141).

Thomas of Celano also repeats this incident in his second biography of Francis. He includes it as one of a whole series of stories under the heading "The Saint's Understanding of Scripture and the Power of his Words," which he introduces as follows:

Although this blessed man was not learned in scholarly disciplines, still he learned from God wisdom from above and, enlightened by the splendors of eternal light, he understood Scripture deeply. His genius, pure and unstained, penetrated hidden mysteries. Where the knowledge of the teacher is outside, the passion of the lover entered. He sometimes read the Sacred Books, and whatever he once put into his mind he wrote indelibly in his heart. His memory took the place of books, because, if he heard something once, it was not wasted, as his heart would mull over it with constant devotion. . . . *Unskilled in words*, he spoke splendidly with understanding and power.[25]

Where do we go to discover this profound theology of Francis? Obviously, we must turn to his own writings, an effort that has begun only over the last twenty-five years.[26] As McGinn accurately summarizes:

Despite the considerable body of research that has been produced on Francis's writings in recent years, it is still difficult to present any synoptic view of his theology. Deceptively simple at first glance, the apparently verbal poverty of his writings, especially the prayers, hides unusual theological riches. What is most striking is the difference between Francis the writer and Francis the saint as portrayed by the biographers.[27]

We are beginning to be conscious of the fact that the images created by the subsequent hagiographic tradition—Francis as the perfect imitator of Christ, for example—were so strong that they have

[25]2C 102 (*FA: ED* 2: 314-315).
[26]This effort was sparked by the call of the Second Vatican Council for religious orders to return to the charism of their founders, but really got under way after the publication of a critical edition of Francis's writings by Kajetan Esser in 1976.
[27]McGinn, *Flowering*, 51.

shaped the lens through which we have read Francis's writings. The challenge for us today is to remove this lens and let Francis's words speak with renewed freshness.

Certainly, Francis did not leave us a large body of writings. The present critical edition contains some thirty works—mainly prayers and letters. With the exception of the two versions of his Rule and the Office of the Passion, they are all quite brief. And yet this modest corpus, containing fewer than one hundred and fifty pages of an average size book, is significant when one considers that other prominent medieval figures have left even less. For example, only one letter of Francis's contemporary, Dominic, a well-educated priest and noted preacher, has survived. This suggests that Francis's brothers made some effort to preserve and collect his writings. Even though most of these are in Latin, they may be classified as examples of vernacular theology. As a layman possessing only an elementary education, Francis's Latin syntax is rudimentary, sometimes awkward, and even incorrect. It is evident, in contrast to Scholastic and monastic authors, that he thought in Italian and then attempted to express his ideas in Latin. But despite this simple language and the occasional nature of his writings, scholars agree that they manifest a remarkably coherent vision of God and creation.

Thaddée Matura has presented the most thorough analysis of this vision, and suggests two texts that may be taken as a key to unlocking it. These are the *Later Admonition and Exhortation* (formerly known as the *Second Letter to All the Faithful*) and chapter 23 of the *Earlier Rule* of 1221.[28] The first thing that one immediately notices about Francis's theological vision in these two writings is its profoundly Trinitarian character. Certainly, God is on every page of Francis's writings, permeating his entire experience, the ultimate reality from whom everything comes and towards whom everything converges. Yet, for Francis, God is not an abstract divine force; he always views and proclaims God as Triune. Francis relates to God as Trinity.[29]

The language he uses to describe God is deeply rooted in traditional Biblical and liturgical sources, somewhat out of step with both contemporary theological and devotional trends. Matura has aptly

---

[28]Thaddée Matura, *Francis of Assisi: The Message in His Writings*, trans. Paul Barrett (St. Bonaventure, NY: The Franciscan Institute, 1997), 33. McGinn also notes Matura's work (*Flowering*, 135).

[29]Matura, 53.

characterized it as "archaic."[30] Indeed, Francis's "God-language" is a prime example of how his own theological perspectives are different from modes of expression that would characterize later Franciscan popular devotional language. Let us compare two Franciscan texts that take their inspiration from the same Biblical passage—Jesus' command to love God above all things. The first is from the conclusion of Bonaventure's devotional treatise, *The Tree of Life*:

> Believing, hoping and loving *with* my *whole heart, with* my *whole mind, and with* my *whole strength*, may I be carried to you, beloved Jesus, as to the goal of all things, . . . for you, my good Jesus, are the redeemer of the lost, the savior of the redeemed, the hope of exiles, the strength of laborers, the sweet solace of anguished spirits, . . . the abundant fountain of all graces, *of whose fullness we have all received.*[31]

The second is from a text to which we have already alluded, chapter 23 of Francis's earlier version of the *Rule*, which contains a close equivalent to this passage:

> *With our whole heart, our whole soul, our whole mind, with our whole strength* and fortitude, with our whole understanding, . . . let us *all love the Lord God*, who has given and gives to each one of us our whole body, our whole soul, and our whole life, who has created, redeemed, and will save us by His mercy alone, who did and does everything good for us.[32]

Both are popular writing aimed at a wide audience, as opposed to technical academic works. But what differences do we see? The most obvious difference is the tone. Bonaventure has expressed himself in the language of the warmly affective personal piety increasingly dominant in the twelfth and thirteenth centuries. In contrast, Francis's language, although enthusiastic, remains much more objective; in Matura's term, it is "archaic," adhering more to traditional liturgical style. Like the liturgy, Francis verbalizes his prayer as "we" rather than "I."

---

[30]As cited by McGinn, *Flowering*, 51, who also recognizes the Trinitarian framework of Francis's thought.

[31]*Tree of Life*, 48. Translated by Ewert Cousins, in *Bonaventure, The Soul's Journey into God, the Tree of Life, the Life of St. Francis* (New York: Paulist Press, 1979), 173.

[32]ER, 23: 8 (*FA; ED*, 1: 84).

Furthermore, Bonaventure's thoughts are directed to Jesus, whereas Francis instinctively prays to God, who for him is always Trinity—Creator, Redeemer, and Savior. Although Christians often "attribute" these works to the specific persons of the Trinity, Francis always envisions the three persons of God as working together in all of them. For example, he does not consider the work of redemption to be the work of the Son alone. It is God the Father who initiates human redemption by speaking his eternal Word, his Son, in the person of Christ to reveal in his life and dying the depth of his love for humankind. The Son in turn sends the Spirit to enliven that love within human hearts.[33] And so, if God is Triune, we have a three-fold relationship to God. As Francis exults in the *Later Exhortation:*

Oh, how glorious and holy and great to have a Father in heaven! Oh, how holy, consoling, beautiful and wonderful to have such a Spouse! Oh, how holy and how loving, gratifying, humbling, peace-giving, sweet, worthy of love, and above all things desirable it is to have such a Brother and such a Son, our Lord Jesus Christ![34]

Francis sees three relationships here: we are the *children* of the heavenly Father, the *brothers and sisters* of Christ, and the *spouses* of the Holy Spirit. Each of these tells us something about Francis's theological vision.

"Oh, how glorious and holy and great to have a Father in heaven!" What is it to experience oneself as a child? Is it not to acknowledge that I am not the source of my own existence, to know in my guts that I was "knit together in my mother's womb, . . . made in secret and woven in

---

[33]For a discussion of Francis's understanding that all three persons of the Trinity are intimately involved in the works of creation, redemption, and salvation, see the pioneering study of Norbert Nguyen-Van-Khanh, *The Teacher of His Heart: Jesus Christ in the Thought and Writings of St. Francis,* trans. Ed Hagman (St. Bonaventure, NY: The Franciscan Institute, 1994), 59-87. As Nguyen observes in connection with the work of redemption: "It is true that Francis had an enormous compassion for Christ crucified, as his biographers unanimously assert. But the tendency to exaggerate this sentiment runs the risk of making us think that Francis restricted his attention solely to our Redeemer's sorrowful Passion. This is not an isolated event but is situated in a long history [of salvation]" (86). It is evident that the Father initiates the act of redeeming humankind from both 2LtF 4 and ER 23, 3 *(FA: ED,* 1: 46, 82). Here we see one of the major "differences between Francis the writer and Francis the saint as portrayed by the biographers" noted earlier by McGinn.

[34]2LtF 54-56 *(FA: ED,* 1: 49).

the depths of the earth" (Ps. 139)? To be a child is to emerge in this world from another, totally dependent on another for nutrition and protection. Thus, when Francis speaks of "God most High," he attempts to verbalize this radical contingency of his very existence: that the source of his being lies in an ineffable mystery beyond himself. Encapsulating Johannine theology, Francis elsewhere states: "The Father dwells *in inaccessible light. God is Spirit, and no one has ever seen God.*"[35] In chapter 23 of the *Earlier Rule*, Francis enumerates some of the "negative" attributes of this unseen God: "without beginning and end, unchangeable, invisible, indescribable, ineffable, incomprehensible, unfathomable." But then, paradoxically, Francis suddenly switches into in a litany of "positive" attributes: "gentle, loveable, delightful, totally desirable above all else."[36] What is the reason for this? Even though he is profoundly aware that "no human being is worthy to pronounce God's name,"[37] Francis is also convinced that this ineffable God has chosen to enflesh his Word, making the depths of the divine mystery known in the person of Christ. Through Christ we know that "God is love"—"Father." We also know that it was through the same Word that was expressed in Christ that "all things came to be."[38]

Thus Francis came to view everything in his life as fashioned in love by an all-good God. As Joseph Chinnici has so aptly expressed it, Francis "experiences God as transcendence *precisely in God's goodness.*"[39] This "all-powerful, most holy, almighty and supreme God" is also "all good, every good, the true and supreme good, . . . who has created, redeemed, and will save us by his mercy alone, who did and does everything good for us."[40] What good did God do for Francis? Literally, "everything"! Looking back at his life, Francis could see that "the Lord *gave me* to begin doing penance, . . . *gave me* faith in churches, . . . *gave me*, and *gives me* still, faith in priests, . . . *gave me* brothers, . . . *has given*

[35]Adm 1.5 (*FA: ED*, 1:128). He cites here 1Tim 6:16, Jn. 4: 24, and Jn. 1:18.
[36]ER 23: 11 (*FA: ED*, 1: 86). Indeed, Francis gives over fifty attributes of God in this one chapter. See also his Praises of God, composed on Mount La Verna after his experience of the Stigmata, which is an uninterrupted paean of positive attributes of the all-good God (*FA: ED*, p. 109).
[37]ER 23.5; CtC 2 (*FA: ED*, 1: 82, 113).
[38]1Tim 6:16, Jn. 4:24, 1:18.
[39]"Evangelical/Apostolic Tensions," in *Our Franciscan Charism in the World Today*, ed. Alcuin Coyle (Clifton, NJ: Franciscan Advertising and Media Enterprises, 1987), 106.
[40]ER 23.1, 9, 8 (*FA: ED*, 1: 83-85). On this theme, see Matura, 53-56.

me to speak and write the Rule."[41] For Francis, everything was the gift of an utterly transcendent, unfathomable, but loving source.

Matura emphasizes several points in this connection that indeed link Francis with the subsequent Franciscan theological tradition. First, he emphasizes "the Father" as having a certain primacy within the Trinity, as the primordial source of the other persons. The overflowing goodness of God is evident first in God's inner life. The Father is the one who expresses self generously and totally.[42] Interestingly enough, when Francis calls God "Father," he does not associate this title primarily with reference to us, but as "Father of our Lord Jesus Christ." The first person of the Trinity is "Father" because his goodness eternally begets a Son. This is why for Francis, Christ is always "the beloved Son." If we are God's "sons" and "daughters," it is because we are incorporated into a relationship that already exists at the very heart of God.[43]

Second, every created thing reveals the goodness of this loving God. "Through your holy will . . . you have created everything spiritual and corporal. . . . Therefore we give you thanks for everything."[44] Francis best captures this insight in the *Canticle of the Creatures*, which McGinn considers his most strikingly creative contribution as a vernacular theologian.[45] The *Canticle* is truly vernacular, and not simply because it is the earliest surviving religious poem in the emerging Italian language. The fact that Francis wanted this poem to remain in Italian and composed music for it demonstrated his intention to communicate a distinctive experience of God to everyone.

After Francis evokes, once again, the transcendence of God "most High," he turns to praise God with (*cum*) and through (*per*) his creatures. Scholars have drawn attention to the unusual passive imperative construction he employs here—e.g., "Be praised my Lord through Sister Water." It indicates that Francis is not simply inviting all creatures to praise God—as in the Biblical pattern of the Canticle of the Three Young Men from the book of Daniel that was a familiar part of

---

[41]Test 1, 4, 6, 14, 39 (*FA: ED*, 124-127).
[42]This theme would be highly developed by Bonaventure. For an introduction, see Ilia Delio, *Simply Bonaventure: An Introduction to His Life, Thought, and Writings* (Hyde Park, NY: New City Press, 2001), 39-45. For the primacy of the Father in Francis's thought, see Matura, 57-61.
[43]Nguyen, 133-141.
[44]ER 23: 1, 5 (*FA: ED*, 1: 82-83).
[45]*Flowering of Mysticism*, 54-56.

the Church's Liturgy of the Hours. Instead, Francis is calling on human beings to praise God *because* and *by means of* the wonderful creatures God has created—all of which manifest God's glory in their unique ways. Each creature is praiseworthy for three different reasons: it is beautiful in itself, it reflects something of God's own nature, and it is good for human beings. Through his use of the terms "brother" and "sister" to describe all created things—even the terrifying reality of bodily death—Francis "enfraternizes" the whole created world. All things manifest a single harmonious theophany of their source, the all-good God. God's presence is expressed as luminously real and immediate in the cosmos as a whole and in each of its elements insofar as they reflect some aspect of the divine fullness.[46]

"Oh, how holy and how loving, gratifying, humbling, peace-giving, . . . and above all things desirable it is to have such a Brother, . . . our Lord Jesus Christ, who laid down his life for his sheep."[47] Traditionally, Franciscan theology and spirituality has been described as Christocentric.[48] In a particular way, Francis is depicted in many of the biographical sources as fascinated by the details of Christ's human life—his birth in the stable of Bethlehem, his itinerant preaching ministry, and especially his Passion and death. But once again, when we turn to Francis's own writings, the role of Christ appears in quite a different light. The elements we have just described are certainly evident, but they are placed within a much deeper and, if you will, more theological context. This context, as already noted, is the mystery that God is Trinity.

As Matura points out, the most striking thing we notice about Francis's own theology is that he speaks about Christ much less than he does about God as Father. And when Francis does speak about Christ at any length, he always does so in the context of the whole Trinity or in relation to the Father.[49] We cannot lose sight of the fact that for Francis

---

[46]*Flowering of Mysticism*, 55. Cf. Roger D. Sorrell, *St. Francis of Assisi and Nature: Tradition and Innovation in Western Christian Attitudes toward the Environment* (New York: Oxford University Press, 1988), who discusses the Canticle in chaps. 5-7 (on "enfraternization," see 127-130).

[47]2LtF 56 (*FA: ED*, 1: 49).

[48]E.g., Eric Doyle: "If there is one word which does complete justice to Franciscan theology and spirituality it is 'Christocentric,' and they have this as their distinguishing feature. . . ." Cf. Eric Doyle, "St. Francis of Assisi and the Christocentric Character of Franciscan Life and Doctrine," in *Franciscan Christology*, ed. Damian McElrath (St. Bonaventure, NY: Franciscan Institute Publications, 1980), 2.

[49]Matura, 62-64.

Christ is always the Son, the Word and self-expression of the Father.[50] A strongly Johannine understanding of the mystery of Christ is evident here. "Through your only Son you have created everything spiritual and corporal. . . ." The Word of God is first of all for Francis the eternal self-expression of the Father in light of which he made all things. But the principle of creation has also become the principle of re-creation: "for as through your Son you created us, so through your holy love with which you loved us you brought about his birth as true God and true man."[51] The Father has chosen to express his own Word as a poor fragile creature among other such creatures in the person of Jesus.[52] In Christ, God has become our brother. Christ then is the Word of God embodied in space and time. Taking our human nature, he makes his own flesh and blood the language through which the Father's total love for his brothers and sisters is expressed. "Let us therefore hold on to the words, the life, the teaching, the holy Gospel of the one who humbled himself to beg his Father for us and to make known his name to us."[53]

"Brother"—this word denotes two important facets of Francis's experience of Christ. First, truly being a "brother" or "sister" to another means I must accept the other, precisely as *other*, as equally an expression of the creative love of my parents. The transcendent mystery in which I discover my own origin has also let these other beings exist. I therefore must accept them in love. And so, by taking our human nature from Mary, Christ became our "brother" by accepting and embracing us as we are in our sinful human "frailty" and "wretchedness."[54] But being a "brother" for Francis also implies the consequences of being a member of the same family. Solidarity with and compassion for humanity impels Christ to move out of himself to "lay down his life for his brothers" (and sisters).[55]

---

[50]Nguyen, 132-141. Again, this was also a basic motif of Bonaventure's thought. Cf. Delio, 46-48.

[51]ER 23.1, 3 (*FA: ED*, 82).

[52]Cf. 2LtF 4: "The most high Father made known from heaven through his holy angel Gabriel this Word of the Father in the womb of the Virgin Mary, from whose womb he received the flesh of our humanity and frailty. Though he was rich, he wished . . . . to choose poverty in the world beyond all else" (*FE: ED*, 1: 46).

[53]ER 22.41 (*FA: ED*, 1: 81).

[54]2LtF 4; ER, 23.5, 8 (*FA: ED*, 1: 46, 82, 84).

[55]2LtF 6-13 (*FA: ED*, 1: 46). It is interesting that when Francis cites Jn. 15:13 ("No one has greater love than this, than to lay down his life for one's friends"), he changes "friends" to "brothers" (Adm 3: 9 [*FA: ED*, 1: 130]). No doubt Francis was also thinking of 1Jn. 3:16: "We know God's love in this, that Christ laid down his life for us, and we

And so Francis views the one person Jesus Christ in terms of his two natures. On the one hand, when Francis contemplates Jesus, who humbled himself to dwell among us, who poured out his blood for us, he sees embodied the depths of the compassion and overflowing love that are the very heart of God. But on the other hand, when he looks at Jesus, Francis comes to recognize his own call as "a brother." For Christ is not simply the expression of God's love in human form, but also reveals how human beings can fulfill our own created destiny to "be like" God, actualizing the deepest dimensions of what we too were called to be—the children of God. For we can only become children of the Father by following in the pattern of "the beloved Son" who fulfilled the Father's will.[56] As "the first-born of many brothers and sisters," Christ has blazed the trail of faithful discipleship by his self-emptying love. In doing so he "has left us an example that we might follow in his footsteps."[57]

But how? Francis himself tells us when he breaks into prayer at the conclusion of his *Letter to the Entire Order*: "Inwardly cleansed, interiorly enlightened, and set on fire by the love of the Holy Spirit, may we be able to follow the footsteps of your beloved Son." This brings us to one of the most profoundly original contributions of Francis as a vernacular theologian—the image of the Holy Spirit as our spouse. We have seen that in his *Later Admonition and Exhortation*, that Francis praises the Holy Spirit through this image: "Oh how holy, consoling, beautiful, and wonderful to have such a Spouse!" This is the third relationship that Francis calls Christians to actualize with the three persons in God: just as he calls them to be truly "children" of the Father, and "brothers" and "sisters" of Christ, he also calls them to be "wedded" to the Spirit.

This image must have been in the forefront of Francis's imagination, as he uses it in the *Antiphon to the Blessed Virgin* that he prayed fourteen times a day. There he exclaims: "Holy Virgin Mary, . . . among the women born into the world there is none like you. Daughter and servant of the most high . . . Father in heaven, Mother of our most

---

ought to lay down our lives for our brothers [and sisters]." Thus, for Francis, Christ has modeled being a brother, giving his life in solidarity with others in self-sacrificing love.

[56]Cf. 2LtF 52: "We are brothers [to Christ] when we do the will of his Father Who is in heaven" (*FA: ED*, 1: 49). Francis expressed the relationship in prayer in his Office of the Passion; in contrast to many popular votive offices of the time, Francis does not pray *to* the suffering Christ; he utters Psalms *with* the suffering Christ to the Father.

[57]2LtF 10-13 (*FA: ED*, 46).

Holy Lord Jesus Christ, Spouse of the Holy Spirit."[58] In a similar fashion, he uses it in the primitive form of life he gave to Clare and her sisters: "by divine inspiration, you have made yourselves daughters and servants of the Most High King, the heavenly Father, and have espoused yourself to the Holy Spirit."[59] Such terminology was highly unusual. The ascetical tradition had for centuries used marital imagery to capture the spiritual meaning of the consecration of religious women, but had always described them as brides of *Christ.*[60] Francis was certainly aware of the traditional imagery. Why then did he describe not only Mary, Clare, and her sisters, but also all committed Christians, as spouses of the *Spirit*? I believe it was because he wanted to capture in this expression something very basic about our relationship to God.[61]

Again, let us look at the human relationship implied by the word "spouse." What happens—at least ideally—when one person weds another? God's creative plan—reaffirmed by Jesus—is that in marriage "two become one flesh."[62] Two persons, in a very real sense, become one—not that they lose their individuality but that the two become one in love. In fact, this loving union actually brings the individuality of both persons to a heightened level. Is not Francis trying to say that when a person is truly open and responsive to the workings of the Spirit, that person in fact "becomes one" with the Spirit of the Lord? Does not Paul say as much: "Anyone united to the Lord becomes one spirit with him"?[63] If someone is wedded to the Holy Spirit, the Spirit of God penetrates and permeates the deepest reality of what that person is. The Spirit is the love bonding the persons of the Father and Son in the Trinity, and it is that same Spirit that united the human will of Christ to the will of the Father in such a way that they were completely one. To possess the Spirit of the Lord Jesus means that the disciple is drawn into that same relationship. And so if we are open to the power of the Spirit, we will gradually be transformed in such a way that what God desires and what we desire will become more and more one movement of love.

---

[58]OfP, Ant. 2 (*FA: ED*, 1: 141). He recited this antiphon at the beginning and the end of each of the seven hours of the Office of the Passion.

[59]RCl 6.3, trans. Regis Armstrong. *Clare of Assisi: Early Documents* (St. Bonaventure, NY: The Franciscan Institute, 1993), 71-72.

[60]Clare herself uses this traditional imagery. See Jean Leclercq, "St. Clare and Nuptial Spirituality," *Greyfriars Review*, 10 (1996): 171-178.

[61]I have further developed this theme in "The Experience of the Spirit in Our Franciscan Tradition," *The Cord*, 49.3 (1999): 114-129.

[62]Gen. 2:24; Mt. 19:5.

[63]1Cor. 16:16-17.

Francis praises Mary because her radical openness to the working of the Spirit transformed her own will, making it one with God's will—thus bringing about the birth of God's Word in the flesh. But in his Later Exhortation, Francis makes clear that all Christians are called to enter into that same relationship with the Spirit.[64] It is by becoming "spouses of the Spirit" that we too are enabled to accomplish the will of the Father, following in the footsteps of Christ by surrendering ourselves in love for one another. In this way, we too may become the "children of the Father, and the brothers and sisters and mothers" of Christ.

I believe that this insight of Francis is key if we are to grasp fully the traditional Franciscan emphasis on liberty and spontaneity. It is not simply that all things are preciously unique on the natural level by virtue of their creation. Francis's awareness of the working of the Spirit of the Lord led him to realize that individuality was accentuated, not diminished, on the level of the "new creation." As Paul tells us: "Where the Spirit of the Lord is, there is freedom" (2Cor 3:17). The mystery of marital union is constraining but liberating. On the one hand, I, as "spouse," must surrender to the embrace of the Spirit. The paradox is that when God possesses me, I do not become less myself—indeed, I am freed to become more fully, uniquely myself.

Francis came to recognize that it is indeed the Spirit of *God* who dwells in the disciple who is espoused to Him/Her. He thus found it difficult to distinguish what was "the Spirit of the Lord and its holy activity" from the personal decision of the committed follower of Christ. He was always attentive to how "divine inspiration" was leading his brothers and sisters, why the commands of a superior must always bow before "the soul" of the individual, and why he called the Holy Spirit "the general minister" of the Order.[65] Such a realization left Francis at a loss when asked to describe "a good Lesser Brother." He could not give an abstract definition, but only point to the special gifts of the Spirit that the brothers around him embodied—irreplaceable persons who enfleshed the working of God in their own unique ways.[66]

---

[64]As McGinn comments: "It is worth noting that this appeal, containing, if not elaborating upon, the traditional mystical themes of espousal, . . . divine filiation, and the birth of Christ in the soul, appears not in a document directed to the *fraternitas*, but to the whole body of the faithful" (*Flowering*, 52).

[65]ER 2.1, 16.3; LR 10.3, 12.1 (*FA: ED*, 1: 64, 74, 105-106); 2C 193 (*FA: ED*, 2: 371).

[66]2MP 85 (*FA: ED*, 3: 333).

Perhaps the emphasis on the Spirit as "spouse" also enables us to understand better one final dimension of Francis's reference to the Triune God as Creator, Redeemer, and Savior. In his doxology in chapter 23 of the *Earlier Rule*, Francis calls upon his brothers to love the Lord God "who *has* created, redeemed, and *will* save us by his mercy alone." Why the change of tenses here? It is because Francis believed that redemption and salvation are not the same. Our redemption has been definitively accomplished in Christ, but our salvation has yet to be achieved. It is something we await.[67] Why? Because our salvation involves not only the continuing gift of God's love but also our personal response to that love. Yes, Francis called on "miserable and wretched" human beings to put their trust in God's boundless mercy.[68] He did this precisely because he recognized all too well that human beings have the power to say no. We must freely consent, as Mary did, to become "spouses of the Spirit." God's loving plan for us will not be accomplished without our "yes."[69] In this sense, the history of human salvation is still unfolding and full dimensions of the love of God have yet to be revealed.

I hope that this small attempt at breaking open two relatively brief documents have revealed somewhat the depths of Francis's theology—his distinctive understanding of God and God's relation to the world. Although expressed in everyday language, Francis's understanding was indeed profound. Those of us who are familiar with the thought of the "professional practitioners" of theology in the Franciscan intellectual tradition may well have identified a number of intuitive insights of Francis that were later developed in a more systematic way. I certainly believe this can be done.[70] In closing, I would simply indicate one major link. The great Franciscan theologians always considered theology to be a practical science—that is, theology cannot be content with the intellect knowing the truth about God; the will must come to choose God as its true and lasting good.[71] This belief sprang from Francis's deepest conviction. Brother Leo remembered

---

[67]Cf. Nguyen, 78-89.

[68]ER 23.8 *(FA: ED*, 1: 84).

[69]Again, a theme echoed by later Franciscan theologians, e.g. Bonaventure, *Breviloquium*, 5.2-3.

[70]I have attempted to suggest several of these links in the notes.

[71]As expressed by Bonaventure: "This doctrine [theology] exists so that we might become good and be saved, and this is not achieved through bare speculation, but by a disposition of the will" *(Brevil.*, prol., 5). Again, one notices the future tense of "save."

Francis as saying: "A person has only as much knowledge as he or she can put into practice; and a religious is as good a teacher as his or her actions show."[72] Francis believed that we do not really *know* something until our head knowledge penetrates our heart and our guts so that we approach our life in the world in a different way. This is a lesson that he, *simplex et idiota*, taught a professional theologian. Bonaventure, near the end of his final work, *The Conferences on the Six Days of Creation*, reminded his brothers that they were called to a life of study, striving to penetrate the meaning of the Word of God. But he concluded with a warning: "Blessed Francis said that he wanted his brothers to study, but first to practice what they preached. After all, what is the use of knowing a lot, but tasting nothing"?[73] If our Franciscan intellectual tradition has stood for anything, it is that any "scientific study of God and God's relation to the world" must cause us to act differently in that world.[74] That conviction was first enunciated by its founder, a vernacular theologian named Francis of Assisi.

---

[72]AC 105: "Tantum scit homo de scientia quantum operatur, et tantum est religiosus bonus orator quantum operatur" (*FA: ED*, 2: 210, alt).

[73]*Collationes in Hexaemeron*, 22.21 (V).

[74]Alluding to Gerald O'Collins's definition of theology mentioned above.

Chapter Three

BONAVENTURE OF BAGNOREGIO: A PARADIGM FOR FRANCISCAN THEOLOGIANS?

Zachary Hayes, O.F.M.

According to *Webster's Dictionary* the definition of "paradigm" is quite simple. It means "a model or pattern." The *American Heritage Dictionary* says practically the same thing. A paradigm is "an example or model." The *Oxford English Dictionary* has a similar entry. The question before us, then, is the following: Is there such a thing as a model for Franciscan theologians? If so, why? And if so, how would Bonaventure fit into the question? I would like first to consider briefly the matter of approaches to the academic work of the friars in the Middle Ages. This will be followed by comments from a number of authors concerning the style of Bonaventure. Finally, I will offer my own reflections on Bonaventure as a Franciscan theologian in relation to what seems to be the task of theologians in the Church in the present period of history.

In approaching any understanding of the Franciscan theological tradition, my personal thought has been deeply influenced by the work of Philotheus Boehner, O.F.M., ever since he created the remarkable courses on the Franciscan intellectual movement of the Middle Ages back in the 1940s. According to his analysis, if we simply look for a common set of themes shared by the great theologians of the past, we will probably have to conclude that there is no such thing as a Franciscan school. While there are a number of theological themes that appear in major authors, they are dealt with differently, and there seems to be very little agreement among the Franciscan friars on some of the most basic philosophical issues that enter into the shaping of a theology. We need only think of the intellectual distance that separates a Bonaventure from an Ockham to get some sense of what Boehner is saying.

On the other hand, neither does any single friar constitute a Franciscan school. What we commonly speak of as the Franciscan school of the Middle Ages involves a remarkable wealth of personalities and of doctrines. In contrast to the possibility of shared themes,

Boehner suggests four qualities that characterize the work of the great friars of the past. Their work is critical, scientific, progressive, and practical. In Boehner's analysis, each of these words has a very specific meaning; and not all Franciscan scholars reflect all the qualities to the same degree.[1] One way of approaching the work of Bonaventure would be to try to see how these four qualities are reflected in his work. In fact, Boehner does this to some degree in his course notes on Bonaventure.[2] This brings out some interesting characteristics of the work of the Seraphic Doctor, but it is only one approach to the matter.

Hans Urs von Balthasar looks at the work of Bonaventure from quite a different viewpoint. He is not concerned with any analysis of a Franciscan school. His argument has to do rather with something of the distinct personality of Bonaventure's theological work. Here I have in mind the role that Bonaventure plays in Von Balthasar's monumental work, *Herrlichkeit*.[3] After first developing his theory on the meaning of beauty in a remarkable analysis of aesthetics, Von Balthasar presents a number of historical figures whose theological work may be seen as examples of his theory in practice. From the great Golden Age of medieval theology, Von Balthasar's choice is not Thomas Aquinas, but rather Bonaventure. Von Balthasar sees the work of Bonaventure as a pre-eminent example of the aesthetic in theology, and hence presents him in terms of the spiritual and conceptual beauty of his theology.

The beauty which is Bonaventure's concern, according to Von Balthasar, takes a specifically Franciscan form in the mystery of the God who humbles Himself in the incarnation and above all on the cross. The final Word about God and humanity has been uttered on the cross; and the stigmatization of Francis gives expression to all that is involved in that mystery and removes any doubt about the meaning of that divine Word. The cross reveals something of the very heart of God as self-sacrificing love that holds to nothing for itself. Love is that "incomprehensible passing over from itself into what is other than itself."[4] And it was the most profound poverty of spirit that opened

---

[1]"The Spirit of Franciscan Philosophy," *Franciscan Studies*, 2.3 (Sept. 1942): 217ff.

[2]*The History of the Franciscan School*, prt. 2 (St. Bonaventure University, 1944-1947, mimeographed notes), 43ff.

[3]We will cite the English translation: Hans Urs von Balthasar, *The Glory of the Lord: A Theological Aesthetics*, Vol. 2, trans. A. Louth, F. McDonagh, B. McNeil (Ignatius Press/Crossroad, 1984).

[4]Von Balthasar, 359.

Francis to receive and to be transformed by that love. This transformation is so radical that it impresses itself not only in his spirit, but also in his flesh in the form of the stigmatization. The imitation of Christ in total poverty is the imitation of a God who is poor. And the spirituality of the imitation of Christ at its core takes the form of a love that surrenders everything for the sake of the other.

In the analysis of Von Balthasar, this Franciscan doctrine in Bonaventure is not a departure from his understanding of the beautiful. Rather, it is the high point of the Seraphic Doctor's whole teaching about beauty. In the deepest sense, beauty resides in the mystery of that ecstatic love that lies at the heart of the divine mystery and that manifests itself in the many forms of creation and salvation.

> It is love in its incomprehensible passing over from itself into what is other than itself. It is love as the eternal generation of the Son from the Father, and as God's act of creation directed into the nothingness—a passing over that reveals at one and the same time the absolute power and infinite fruitfulness of God and the divine disposition of poverty, that wishes to have and hold on to nothing for itself. This disposition becomes visible in the creation, and more fully in redemption, as a descent into nothingness and fruitlessness."[5]

Von Balthasar uses an interesting image to speak of Bonaventure's relation to Francis. For anyone who has visited Our Lady of the Angels and the Portiuncula, this image will speak volumes. Bonaventure's work, writes Von Balthasar, is a glorious, spiritual cathedral that rises above the unpretentious Portiuncula chapel of Francis of Assisi.[6]

More recently, in a way that seems to bear directly on our topic for today, Klaus Hemmerle[7] has argued that Bonaventure's style of theology suggests a way for contemporary theologians. Bonaventure's theology is in essence a theology of Exodus; of going forth in and with history into God. This is the style so eloquently expressed in the *Itinerarium*. But the idea pervades the entire thought-world of

---

[5]Von Balthasar, 359.
[6]Von Balthasar, 263.
[7]Klaus Hemmerle, *Theologie als Nochfolge: Bonaventura—ein Weg für Heute* (Herder: Freiburg, Basel, Wien, 1975).

Bonaventure. For Hemmerle, it represents a way in which theologians today would be able: "To make God believable, understandable, and alive for people today.[8] In Hemmerle's view, this way would allow theologians to open Christian consciousness to a significant alternative vision contrasting with the shallowness of so much of what goes today as contemporary culture.

In a similar way, Theo Zweerman, O.F.M., highlights the opening of Bonaventure's *Itinerarium*: "Incipit speculatio pauperis in deserto." The poor one! This means, for Bonaventure, the basic significance of spiritual poverty as the starting point for the spirituality of the human journey into God and for the theological reflection which, in the case of Bonaventure, plays such an important role in that journey. As Zweerman sees it, a theology inspired by this vision would stand in remarkable contrast with the ever-increasing consumerism of contemporary culture and could open a vision of meaning in a world where a sense of the deeper meaning of life is seriously lacking.[9]

Each of these approaches offers significant possibilities. All in some way highlight the relation between Francis and Bonaventure. There is no doubt in my mind that the spirituality and theology of Bonaventure are intimately related to the experience of Francis of Assisi. But for now, my intention is not to draw out the implications of this for particular points of doctrine. My concern will be to highlight particular characteristics of Bonaventure's style that may well be seen as paradigmatic for Franciscan theologians today.

Personal Attitude.

I would first pick up the issue I have just mentioned from Zweerman. I would refer to this as Bonaventure's personal attitude toward the intellectual work of theology in which he was engaged so extensively—the "poor one" in the desert as he writes in the *Itinerarium*. But already in his early *Commentary on the Sentences*, he describes himself in the following words: "I know and I confess that I am a poor and needy *compilator*."[10] At first reading, we would be inclined to see this

---

[8]Hemmerle, 11.
[9]Theo Zweerman, OFM, "Prolegomena zur Lektüre von Texten Bonaventuras über das Buch der Schöpfung," *Franziskanische Studien* 71(1989): 29-41.
[10]*II Sent*. Praelocutio (II, 1).

simply as a statement of the medieval style of appealing to the work of the Fathers of the Church and to other writers whose work is seen as authoritative. It was a common practice to draw materials from other authors better than oneself; that is, from the *auctores*. From this perspective, Bonventure sees his work as that of a "compiler." But we could play with that a bit more in terms of the etymology of the Latin word and discover that the work of a compiler may be compared to the work of a robber. This is certainly less complimentary.

However we choose to interpret the Latin, there is no doubt that here a scholar who is considered by both his contemporaries and by later generations to be a great intellectual was keenly aware of his own personal limitations and the limitations of the entire project in which he was involved. Does this speak to us today of the liberating power that a genuine poverty of spirit can have for a person engaged in the intellectual life and of the way in which this poverty of spirit can become a genuine source of fruitfulness for the spiritual life and for the theological reflection of the theologian? And what might this say about the pathetic games that so often become an almost self-evident part of the academic world of today?

Ecclesial Context.

In a situation within the Church and within the Franciscan Order itself where there was considerable controversy and numerous factional groups, Bonaventure begins his final series of collations by citing the text of Ecclesiasticus 15:5: "In the midst of the church, the Lord will open his mouth and fill him with the spirit of wisdom and understanding."[11] Bonaventure uses this text to point to the audience he wishes to address. It is, as we know, largely an audience of friars at the University of Paris. Beyond this, according to F. Delorme, there may have been another hundred and sixty friars in attendance.[12] Bonaventure uses the text to point specifically to their place and his own place within the community of the Church. Theologians must be people of the Church. This is all the more true of Franciscans who are theologians. At

---

[11]*Hex.* I, 2 (V, 329).
[12]*Collationes in Hexaemeron et Bonaventuriana Quaedam Selecta*, ed. F. Delorme (Quaracchhi, 1934), 275.

least four times in one paragraph of this text, Bonaventure speaks of the importance of "harmony" and "concord." The Church is a community of faith bound together by love. A deep sharing in the faith-life of the Church is required for a theologian to find full wisdom and understanding.

Bonaventure's own work as a theologian had not only personal meaning for his spirituality, but it had important implications for mediating between strongly opposed viewpoints among the friars and between some friars and the authorities of the Church. This seems to be especially clear in his final *Collations on the Hexaemeron*. Among other issues, he is concerned with the problems created within the fraternity by the Joachimite movement. A careful reading of these collations indicates that Bonaventure went as far as he could go in addressing their concerns, even assuming some of the language style characteristic of their movement. But he did so in a way that still allowed him to point out what he saw as very dangerous errors in the Joachimite position. Beyond this, Bonaventure also addresses the situation of the academic friars in the audience. This deals specifically with the mission of teaching and preaching in the life of the Church at large. He offers a way of justifying the pastoral mission of the Order in response to both the internal and the external critics. His work may be seen as an outstanding example of mediation and attempted reconciliation at several critical levels for the life of the Order and the life of the Church.

One might think of the implications of this approach as a possible model for theologians today in relation to the conflicts found pervasively among Franciscans about issues of life-style and ministry and at virtually every level in the life of the Church as a whole. How can one be concerned seriously with the Christian tradition and with one's personal appropriation of that tradition and, at the same time, address the diversity in the life of the Church that cries out for some form of mediation?

A Wisdom Style.

Bonaventure's work is widely recognized as one of the outstanding medieval examples of what is called a "wisdom style" of reflection. By this we mean that his major concern is not simply to develop abstract philosophical concepts, distinctions, and proofs about matters that may or may not be important, but rather to deal more concretely with the questions related to the meaning of human life. How are such questions to be dealt with in the context of the relations that human persons build with each other, with the world of nature, and with God?

Here Bonaventure demonstrates a style in which the personal development of faith and the creative reflection on faith are able to interact and mutually enrich each other. It is a style that relates spiritual practice with theological knowledge. The dynamism of this approach stands out especially in miniature masterpieces such as the *Itinerarium* and the *De reductione artium*. In these two works we see a vision that draws all the arts and sciences into the human, spiritual journey to the final goal of human life and cosmic history.

Several issues stand out here. First is the place of the arts in education and in the unfolding of the spiritual life. Most of our educational centers have taken some form of a liberal arts program as basic to their style. But more and more, this is being questioned in relation to the possibility of more professional programs. It is certainly clear that people have to make a living. But it is especially obvious today that people also need to live a life. Certainly the richness communicated by a good program in the arts can interact in a significant way with the sense of meaning and purpose communicated through religious faith and theology. In that sense, such an interaction can provide the basis from which people can engage in a life-long journey of spiritual, intellectual development.

Beyond this, there is the question of engaging the positive sciences. The present Holy Father has spoken about the need for some form of conversation between theology and the sciences.[13] The sciences as we know them today are very different from anything that would have been seen as science in the Middle Ages. But the task of engaging theology in a critical and creative conversation with them may turn out to be crucial for the future of the human race. The wisdom-style of Bonaventure suggests the possibility of a more holistic form of humanism. Bonaventure himself was able to bring together faith and reason, mysticism and rationality, as well as experience and tradition not as opposites but as mutually enriching dimensions of the theological

---

[13]Cf. *Physics, Philosophy, and Theology: A Common Quest*, ed. R. J. Russell, W. R. Stoeger, G. Coyne (Vatican Observatory and Notre Dame Press, 1988).

project. The challenge of doing something comparable for our world today is crucial. His project challenges us to engage all the arts and sciences of our time with the religious, theological concerns of the believer.

A Critical Style.

Boehner has spoken of the critical quality of the Franciscan tradition. When we hear the word "critical," we might be inclined to think more quickly of Scotus and Ockham than of Bonaventure. And indeed, they were critical at a level that would probably have been impossible for Bonaventure. But in its own way, and perhaps at a different level, the work of Bonaventure is critical as well.

We see this first in terms of his relation to his early theological master, Alexander of Hales. While Bonaventure certainly has great respect for Alexander, his own work is not simply a repetition of his predecessor's. Bonaventure carries the task of theology to a new level. Beyond this, he was quite well aware of the quality of the philosophical work of both Plato and Aristotle. He is able to point out what were the strengths and weaknesses of these two giants of Greek antiquity. In a well-known Christological sermon, he compares the epistemologies of the two great Greek philosophers in terms of their strengths and their weaknesses.[14] Elsewhere he could refer to Aristotle as the "prince and leader of the Peripatetics."[15] But he does not hesitate to point out where certain philosophical positions of Aristotle stand in contradiction to truths of the Christian faith. We have in mind here especially the problem of the eternity of the world and the denial of individual immortality. Beyond this, Bonaventure is engaged in an ongoing criticism of the secularizing philosophical movement of his own time.

> Against the harmonious praise of God there is a spirit of presumption and curiosity. We take this to mean that the presumptuous person does not glorify God but gives praise to himself, and the curious person does not have a sense of devotion. There are many people of this kind who lack both praise and devotion while they are filled with the splendors of

---

[14]Cf. "Christ the One Teacher of All," *What Manner of Man? Sermons on Christ by St. Bonaventure*, trans. Z. Hayes (Chicago: Franciscan Herald Press, 1974). 37.

[15]*II Sent.* d. 1, p. 1, a.1, q.1, resp. (II, 17).

the sciences. They build wasps' nests without honeycombs, while the bees make honey.[16]

It is hard to reflect on this without recalling the present Holy Father's encyclical on *Faith and Reason*. There the Pope highlights the history of the interaction between faith and reason in Christian experience, and he urges that we move in the direction of a conversation with culture that is both critical and creative. The Pope is speaking specifically of Aquinas as an outstanding example.[17] In his own different way, Bonaventure reflects a similar dynamic. He recognizes the distinction between reason and faith; and he works with this distinction not so much to safeguard the "rights" of reason but rather to keep reason in its own proper place and to recognize the limits of reason.[18] Because philosophy knows nothing of Christ, it cannot come to the deepest knowledge of our true origins, nor to a knowledge of the deepest roots of our human problems—the sinful situation that conditions human experience from the beginning. Hence, philosophy in the world of antiquity never came to an adequate understanding of the goal of human life. We think here again of Aristotle and the denial of eternal life for individuals.

Hence, if we take Bonaventure as an example for Franciscan theologians today, we would expect to see theology and educational efforts fully aware of the positive values of the culture we are dealing with. We would also expect them to be involved in opening the minds of people to possibilities other than some of the major secularizing values that shape our society today.

The Unifying Power of the Center.

The whole of Bonaventure's approach to philosophy and theology is conditioned from the start by a decision of Christian faith that I like to call the *a priori* of all his philosophical and theological reflection. This decision is expressed in a number of places, but nowhere so clearly as in his *Collations on the Hexaemeron*. It is seen also with remarkable

---

[16]*Hex.* I, 8 (V, 330).
[17]*Fides et Ratio*, #43.
[18]*Brevil.* 1, 1 (V, 210).

consistency in the *De reductione artium* and in the *Itinerarium*. At the opening of the *Collations on the Hexaemeron*, Bonaventure tells us emphatically that we must begin our reflections at the center of reality; and that center is Christ.[19] This is the methodological equivalent of what we find in the spirituality of Francis of Assisi. The Poverello was a person of intense religious experience focused strongly on the mystery of Christ. To the best of our knowledge, however, he was not likely to submit his personal experience to a critical assessment.

We who live in the aftermath of Feuerbach, Marx, and Freud are keenly aware of the problems attendant upon any uncritical appeal to religious experience. Does one, in a religious experience, ever break out of the structures of one's own subjectivity? Or is one forever confined within the prison of the self? The fascination that Francis holds for so many is related to the intensity of his religious experience. The importance of a theologian such as Bonaventure may be seen in his willingness to analyze what that religious experience might imply, if it is to be taken not as a mere subjective trick, but as an authentic religious discernment in the power of which Francis came to place himself ever more deeply in harmony with the structures of reality. We have not said enough if we merely eulogize Francis and fail to see that he, like all great religious figures, raises questions of basic significance.

Bonaventure raises the Christ-centered spirituality of Francis to a more conscious and articulate level. This leads Bonaventure's theology to think ever more strongly of Christ as the center of unity of the entire theological project, which becomes clear in the text we have cited above. The power of this unifying center pervades the whole of Bonaventure's systematic theology. One wants to think of the power of this approach in our own time when so many people experience themselves in terms of the brokenness of a fractured existence. Does the Christian faith offer any vision that can help us integrate and unify reality in the search for human meaning?

There will always be an unliveable tension between an uncritical reading of Christian tradition and an uncritical modernity with its strongly secular and humanistic orientation. But it is important to ask whether that tension can be reduced and transformed into a creative power by a critical approach to both poles of the problem. The option

---

[19]*Hex.* I, 1 (V, 329).

of Bonaventure strikes a resonance with contemporary concerns in a number of ways. First, in taking religious experience as its starting point, it is free to use metaphysical insights to explicate that experience. But it need not be limited by any specific metaphysical system. It can search for those metaphysical views that seem to harmonize with its own deepest intuitions. A theology developed from such a base would reflect the larger historical movement of Christian consciousness as a whole. For, as Alfred North Whitehead once wrote, Christianity itself is pre-eminently an historical religious experience in search of its own proper metaphysical understanding. While Christian thought over the centuries has employed a variety of metaphysical resources, it has not as yet adequately articulated the metaphysical implications of its own original experience.[20]

The view of Bonaventure and its elaborate development in his own writings provides a significant case-history of a theologian who has struggled to interpret all dimensions of reality by means of insights and analogies drawn from the crucial historical disclosure from which Christian faith has claimed to live.

A common fear today concerning such a consistent Christ-centered style is that it will inevitably lead to a form of Christian, spiritual imperialism. Though this can and often does happen, it is not the inevitable outcome of a Christ-centered approach. The current discussion about the relation of Christianity to the other great world religions has led to some helpful distinctions. Some hold to an unmitigated pluralism of religions. This is a view laden with its own problems, which we do not intend to discuss here. We simply mention that such a position has major problems with anything like the Christian doctrine about the incarnation in its classical form. Obviously, it would have only a negative estimation of anything approaching Christocentrism. But the distinction between exclusive and inclusive Christocentrism, used by many in inter-religious conversations, is more helpful. The former refers to those views according to which there can be no true knowledge of God, no grace, and no salvation outside of an explicitly Christian context. The latter refers to those views which search out the possibility that what Christians call God, grace, and salvation is—in some way— universally accessible to human experience

---

[20]Alfred North Whitehead, *Adventures of Ideas* (New York: Free Press, 1933), 164ff.

even though it may be differently understood and articulated at different points of history and in different cultures.

Bonaventure's work suggests the possibility of an inclusive Christocentrism for us today. His project, as he himself developed it, culminated in a breath-taking universalism in which all that is truly human finds its proper home in Christ. The integrating power of the Center opens one's vision to all of creation in a way that turns Francis's *Canticle of Creatures* into an all-embracing program. Such an approach could be very helpful for the development of a rich and significant dialogue between Christianity and the other religious traditions of the world. From such a base, one would be able to approach other traditions with the honest expectation of hearing something that resonates deeply with one's Christian convictions.

Conclusion.

Bonaventure points to a way of doing theology that opens the possibility of a fuller, richer expression of humanity. His importance as a paradigm lies not so much in specific doctrines, interesting as they may be, but rather in the way he opens a vision of a life-long, ongoing process of growth and self-refinement. His way enhances our humanity through a continuously deepening knowledge of the world of God's creation and of ourselves in this world. He envisions a dialogue between the human spirit with its orientation toward union with the mystery of God's love and the human, worldly context in which human life must be lived out. Bonaventure's style is of interest not only as a way of coming to understand faith but also as a guide to help us translate faith into life.

When we speak of Bonaventure as a possible paradigm for Franciscans doing theology today, we do not mean that he is the only one of our tradition who could fill such a role. Neither do we suggest a simple reconstruction of his theology, for, like every style of theology, it is deeply contextual and reflects in its inner structure presuppositions that are foreign to modern sensibilities. It seems clear also that Bonaventure was not fully consistent in exploiting the possibilities of his own presuppositions. But he does suggest to us an approach that could liberate our tradition from unnecessary metaphysical restrictions and allow us to develop a theology more appropriate for today in terms of our resources and our presuppositions.

Such an approach could be of great benefit in a number of ways. If, like Bonaventure, we were not to allow a philosophical metaphysics to set the rules of the game, but instead look to the disclosive possibilities of the religious experience centering around the person and history of Jesus, we might come to significant insights concerning the mystery of the sacred and its involvement in human life. That religious experience suggests a divine presence that is quiet, tender, and evocative rather than domineering and controlling. What ways of thinking about God could be developed from such disclosive experiences? This is not a question of rejecting metaphysical inquiry. Rather, it is a question of searching in the disclosure of Jesus' life and destiny for clues as to the nature of God without allowing a foreign metaphysical system to force our hand too soon. A theology worked out from this base would enable Christians to come to a deeper awareness of their own religious genius.

With a fuller awareness of its own nature as a religious vision, Christianity would be better equipped to enter into significant relations with other religious traditions. Without loss of its own identity, Christianity would be able, in the spirit of Vatican II, to affirm those many elements that the major traditions seem to have in common, though each tradition may deal with these differently. Insofar as there are significant differences among the religious traditions, a healthy dialogue will involve also a challenge to distorting elements in all the traditions. Such dialogue can lead to a genuine enrichment of the respective traditions.

As an historical system, the theology of Bonaventure demonstrates the disclosive power of religious experience and the possibility of developing a genuinely metaphysical and mystical vision from such experience. Karl Rahner speaks of a "searching Christology." As we indicated above, Whitehead has described Christianity as an historical religious experience in search of its own proper metaphysical understanding. Both the theologian and the philosopher point to a matter of great importance concerning the nature of the historic Christian faith. It is not a closed and finished system. It is a religious experience in search of a responsible self-understanding. Any closed theological system threatens to destroy this open-ended and ultimately eschatological disclosure.

It is Bonaventure's strength that he has shown with remarkable power the possibility of dealing with religious experience responsibly. The way he does it allows the quiet disclosure of a limited historical experience centering around the person and history of Jesus of Nazareth to unfold into a stunning vision of reality. As Boehner has pointed out: "It is in the fruitful marriage between the divergent tendencies of speculation and charity, science and wisdom, intellectualism and mysticism, with emphasis always on the second part, that St. Bonaventure has found the solution for his personal problem, and that of his Order."[21] Bonaventure's primary concern is that we use every form of knowledge in the right spirit and for the right purpose. That is to say, we must learn to join knowledge with charity. "Scientia inflat, caritas aedificat; ideo oportet iungere cum scientia caritatem."[22] Knowledge is never an end in itself. It must always become a step toward ever deeper, richer love and transforming union with the God of love.

The heritage of Bonaventure stands as a thought-provoking model for Franciscan theologians of our own time. The issue is not simply to repeat his theological positions, but to do for our time what he did in such a powerful way for his.

---

[21]*The History of the Franciscan School*, prt. 2, p. 43.
[22]*De donis Spiritus Sancti*, IV, 24 (V, 478).

Chapter Four

JOHN DUNS SCOTUS IN THE POSTMODERN, SCIENTIFIC WORLD

Kenan B. Osborne, O.F.M.

Introduction

For many of us living in today's new-millennium world, the so-called real world of our day-to-day existence has several key characteristics. This world is pervasively technological. We can hardly exist without the technological benefits the Western world has gained. Internet, cell phones, automobiles, and airplanes are only a few items that an average person today not only uses but also needs. This world is also pervasively scientific. Health care is highly dependent on science. Agriculture and education are scientifically structured. This world is also called the "postmodern world." Although this phrase has no clear meaning and although it is used much like an umbrella to cover a wide variety of issues, not all compatible with one another, I am using it here to indicate that philosophically, not just technologically and scientifically, there is a definite *epistemé* in the way in which contemporary Western people think.[1]

The Western world has become increasingly secular. Although religion remains an integral part of many Westerners, it is by and large excluded in a deliberate way from politics, education, and almost all forms of the media, business, and social action. Religion has been more and more confined to the private sphere of a person's life. There are, of course, individuals and communal groups who continue to bring religion into public life, but they do so against an anti-religion bias.

Although many Western people will agree that they live in a basically technological, scientific, and secular world, "this world" is far from the total world of contemporary society. The area in which "this

---

[1]The term *episemé* is taken from Michel Foucault, *Les mots et les choses* (Éditions Gallimard: Paris, 1966). I have explained this in my own book, *Christian Sacraments in a Postmodern World*, 57 (Paulist Press: NY, 1999).

world" is a reality involves Europe, England, Ireland, Canada, the United States, Australia, and New Zealand. To some degree "this world" is found in Mexico and in some countries of South America, as well as in the cosmopolitan parts of Russia. Outside of "this world" lie Central America and Asia in its totality, including Sri Lanka and India. Taiwan, Singapore, and South Korea might be seen as exceptions. Most of the countries in Africa and the islands off the African shore do not live in "this world." By far, the vast majority of people do not live in the scientific, technological, and secular world. The so-called Western world of science, technology, and secularism is the "real world" for only a small percentage of the human race. Nor can it be said that this form of "real world" is accepted as the benchmark for all other worldviews. This Western "real world" involves only a minor percent of the earth's population.

Nonetheless, this so-called "real world" presents a major issue, namely, the relationship of science and technology in all their forms with religion. The question that continually arises is this—is religion even meaningful in today's scientific and technological world? The majority of those involved in science and technology are not anti-religion. They are, rather, indifferent and at times neutral. Religion, for them, is not an integral part of their scientific and technological endeavors. Here again one encounters a privatization of religion. In the public spheres of science and technology, just as in the public spheres of politics, economics, and education, religion is not an operative factor. This has led some Western people to ask whether religion and science are even compatible.

Among postmodern philosophers, novelists, poets, and artists, there are indeed some who are belligerently against any and all forms of religious thinking. Gabriel Vahanian, some years ago, wrote a book, *Wait Without Idols.*[2] In a fascinating way he analyzes contemporary novels from North America to Sweden. In this analysis he describes the obsolescence of God. From the first period of these novels to the last period, one can see a movement towards an increasing disregard of religion. He begins with Nathaniel Hawtorne's *The Scarlet Letter*, in which religion is evident but already under criticism. He moves through William Faulkner's *The Sound and the Fury*, T. S. Eliot's *Four Quartets*, and ends with Par Lagerkvist's *Barabbas*. These novels witness to the

---

[2]Gabriel Vahanian, *World Without Idols* (George Brasiller: New York, 1964).

decreasing relevance of God that characterizes religion's relationship to contemporary culture.

Religious leaders have tried, during the last two centuries, to present a credible case for religion. Both Christian and Jewish leaders have played a major part in these attempts. Islamic leaders, by and large, have not been involved in such endeavors. For the Islamic world, religion remains an essential part of all facets of life, including politics, economics, and education. An attempt to create a secular Islamic world has only brought about major clashes. In the Hindu world the situation is almost the same. For many Asian countries such as China, Korea, Taiwan, Thailand, Myamar, Laos, Cambodia, Vietnam, Japan, and the Philippines, forms of Confucian, Daoist, and Buddhist worldviews remain distinctively active. The so-called Asian worldview is profoundly different from the so-called Western worldview.

In the Christian and Jewish attempts to make religion acceptable to the scientific, technological, and secular majority in the West, biblical and scientific writings have been analyzed and interpreted in ways that highlight common factors. Religious leaders have described positive relationships between religion and science. Christian evangelists have attempted to make Jesus and his message a center of contact for the deeper desires of scientists and technologists. An appeal has been made to the profound values of human life and not simply to the intellectual and pragmatic clarity of science and technology. Jewish leaders have used the Holocaust with its religious implications as a continuous call to both science and technology not to disregard profoundly human values as well as deeply treasured religious values. The humanization and spiritualization of both science and technology is, in this Jewish view, a "must." Otherwise, a recurrence of the "Holocaust" remains menacingly possible.

The efforts of both Christian and Jewish leaders in this regard are based on a major religious position, namely, belief in God or in some form of transcendence. God may not always be center stage in their presentations, but the issue of God and God's relationship to both science and technology remains the most basic and fundamental issue, rather than Jesus or the Holocaust. Religions are based on God or on some form of transcendence. Is such a basis needed for contemporary science and technology? Is it even compatible with a postmodern world?

Rather than present a picture of Jesus in Franciscan theology and this theology's value for science and technology, I wish to focus only on the God/science issue, since this is key today. Only on the basis of a theo-anthropology or a theo-cosmology is either Jesus or the Holocaust truly meaningful. In this essay, then, I will argue that elements of John Duns Scotus's thought offer a strong linkage, both philosophically and theologically, to today's scientific and technological realities and their possible relation to the God issue. Several of Scotus's philosophical positions, which are generally not the philosophical positions of mainstream Christian thought, are of key value to contemporary science. The influence of these philosophical positions on theology, again a theology that is generally not the theological position of mainstream Christian thought, are also of valuable assistance to contemporary science and technology.

In the development of this essay, I would like to stress once more that the God-issue must be clarified first in the God/science discussion, since not every interpretation and presentation of God is credible today. Before any talk of Jesus or the Holocaust, the issue of God/science must be addressed. Since there is in the Jesus presentations and in the Holocaust presentations some theology of God, this does not mean that these theologies of God are credible to today's scientist. If the God-issue is not faced first, no other religious issues are truly viable.

Contemporary Life and the Meaningfulness of "God"

For thousands of years men and women have celebrated, worshipped, and prayed to God. Books of prayers to God and rituals celebrating the presence of God in this world are singularly extensive. Thousands, if not millions, of theological and religious books have been written over these past millennia. Scholars, kings, and ordinary people have pressed for their "view of God." Even wars over religion have been waged, some fierce and some less destructive. One cannot write a history of the human race without giving a major place of honor to humanity's belief in God, the ritual expression of this belief, and theological discussions about God. In this new millennium, things are not different. Today, prayers and rituals, celebrations and worship continue in a strong way throughout the world. To speak of the contemporary world as secular or atheistic is myopic. Roughly three-fourths of today's population are religious, believing in God or in a transcendent being. In some major parts of the Western world, there is a deliberate silence about God. This is most evident in the media, in politics, in education, in medicine, and, for some, in their very style of life. Contemporary analyses of economic situations, legislative debates on key issues of societal life, political endeavors for a globalized world omit, more often than not, any indication, even a brief nod, that the issues of religion and God might play any role in human life. Mention of God or religion in these areas is quickly dismissed on the basis that it is irrelevant.

Today's atheistic, postmodern philosophers strongly present their negative positions about God. Generally, however, their rejection of God is a rejection of a particular, most likely Western, presentation about God. Factually speaking, it is no simple matter to say, "there is no God" or "God cannot exist." When people speak this way, one legitimately asks: Which God are they denying? Is it a Christian understanding of God? or an Islamic understanding of God? or a Hindu understanding of God? or a Jewish understanding of God? Atheistic writers may think they are denying every human presentation of God. However, when their positions are carefully analyzed, they are really denying a certain presentation about God. For example, Marx's atheistic writings denied a Western, even Lutheran, understanding of God. Freud's atheistic writings denied a Western, Jewish understanding of God.

John Wright points to another twentieth-century discussion on God:

In the last two decades, beginning with Radical Theology or the Death of God movement, not only has the validity of the word "God" been denied, but its actual meaning has been called into question. That is, not only is it maintained that the word has no objective referent in reality, but that it has no real meaning for human intelligence; it is said to be defined by a series of words and images that are not ultimately grounded in human experience, and is therefore finally meaningless. One cannot talk meaningfully about a maker of the world if one does not experience any such claim. One cannot speak intelligibly about the one who guides history unless one experiences that history is in fact guided. Thus all the conventional ways of understanding the word "God" are said to be groundless.[3]

In the writings of Nietzche, Sartre, and Merleau-Ponty, there is a struggle with the "God question." Each in his own way rejects not just God but a more specific description of God. In his book, *Phenomenology · and Atheism*, William Luijpen notes that if there is today a recalling of God for these philosophers and their followers, it will be a recalling of God in some different and clearer form.

> Modern man, then, will not, without more ado, call God back, when the time for it has arrived. Jupiter and Thor, after their fall, have never been restored to their altars, and rightly so. So also will the man of the future not call back a "God" who has to make up, as a sort of physical energy, for the loss of energy in the macrocosm, who has to justify the injustices of the mighty of this world, who makes the poor accept their wretched lot on earth. . . . He will not be a God who acts like a French king or a German emperor. . . . He will not be a God who lets theologians have a look at the maps of his Providence. . . . With the heaven above his head empty of pseudo-gods, he [modern man] will walk through the world and history, calling for a Transcendent God.[4]

On the other hand, even with the passage of thousands of years of human history in which God or the transcendent have played a significant role, there has never been and there is not today an understanding of God that is universally accepted. Most likely no understanding of God can or will be one which the majority of men and women in this world accept. Various religions and their theologies have offered in the past and still offer today a wide range of descriptions on the meaning of God. In the West a definition of God as the Supreme Being has often been used as the fundamental notion of God. However, the use of the term "being" with all its philosophical implications involves a complex, Western understanding of the world, based on a

---

[3]John H. Wright, "God," *The New Dictionary of Theology*, ed. J. Komonchak et al., (Michael Glazier: Wilmington, DE, 1987), 424.
[4] William J. Luijpen, *Phenomenology of Atheism* (Duquesne University Press: Pittsburgh, 1964), 336-337.

philosophy of being. Many cultures are philosophically not grounded in a "being world."

The contemporary, Western denial of the existence of God, which is at times based on some postmodern philosophies and on scientific and technical investigations, remains a major issue. In the present retrieval of our traditions in Franciscan philosophy and theology, I believe that there are in the Franciscan tradition, especially in philosophy, remarkable affinities to positions on God-related issues, both positive and negative, as presented by contemporary physical scientists, postmodern philosophers, and philosophically interested literary authors. In making this connection of Franciscan philosophy to new millennium thought, I do not intend to transpose a medieval framework on today's quite different ideational framework. Only key philosophical processes, methods, and insights from the Franciscan tradition are transferable.

However, in the current retrieval of Franciscan traditions, there is an issue that needs to be clearly addressed. Franciscan traditions in both theology and philosophy cannot be limited to our Western world. A far more difficult task in this retrieval stems from the multi-cultural world in which we live. The Franciscan missionaries of the past followed the general procedures for most Roman Catholic missionaries. They brought a Western religion with its Western theology, its liturgy, and its philosophical infrastructure to South America, Central America, Mexico, the United States, and Canada. The same is true for Africa and Southeast Asia. Without censuring this method of missionary activity, I believe that the present retrieval of our Franciscan traditions must face other cultures in a different way. For example, do our Franciscan traditions have any contemporary relevance to any of the Buddhist traditions? We cannot answer this question without studying the very meaning of Buddhist tradition. In inter-religious dialogues, Roman Catholic delegates too often communicate with experts in other religions with a fundamental, often unspoken, presupposition that the Roman Catholic religion is the paragon of all religions. Other religions, though partially good, remain defective and misleading. In the efforts we make for a Franciscan retrieval, we must let ourselves learn from other cultures. We may discover that their views require us to reconstruct our own Franciscan thinking in a quite radical way. In this essay I do not make any effort to consider our Franciscan tradition in the framework of another culture; I am merely saying that this task remains to be done.

With these caveats in mind, I would like to explore how major and pivotal issues in the Franciscan tradition can be transferred to our contemporary Western discussion and how this can be done in a highly productive and advantageous way.

The Franciscan Tradition and Today's Philosophical Ethos

In the late twelfth century, John Duns Scotus deliberated on the possibility of knowing who and what God is in ways that are akin to contemporary questions on who and what God is.[5] Evidence for this connection comes from contemporary philosophers themselves. Several postmodern authors have recently written on the philosophical thought of Scotus, indicating the relevance of their own postmodern ideas with those of this medieval man.[6] Scotus's position on the possibility of the human intellect to have access to God without any revelation, using only its own natural abilities, is a key area of affinity.[7] Scotistic scholars have debated whether the text first appeared in the *Ordinatio* and later in the *Tractatus* or vice versa.[8] Contemporary scientists and philosophers operate in a way that parallels Scotus's endeavor—to study an issue using only the natural talents of the human mind. This, I believe, is a major connection between modern science and the Franciscan tradition as evidenced in the *Tractatus* of Scotus. In our current Western world, we might phrase the question as follows: what

---

[5] Scotus, *Tractatus de primo principio*, Latin and English texts in *A Treatise on God as First Principle*, trans. and ed. with a commentary by Allan B. Wolter, O.F.M. (Franciscan Herald Press: Chicago, 1968).

[6] Cf. for example: Gustav Bergmann, *Logic and Reality* (University of Madison Press: Madison, WI, 1964); idem, *Meaning and Existence* (University of Madison Press: Madison, WI, 1968); W. Park, "Scotus, Frege and Bergmann," *The Modern Schoolman*, 67 (1972): 259-273; David Armstrong, *Nominalism and Realism* (Cambridge University Press: Cambridge, 1980); R. M. Chisholm, "Possibility Without Haecceity," *Studies in Essentialism*, ed. Peter French et al. (Minneapolis, 1986); G. S. Rosenkrantz, *Haecceity: An Ontological Essay* (Dordrecht, 1933); O. Boulnois, "Genèse de la théorie scotiste de l'individuation," *Le problème de l'individuation*, ed. A. Pitpohl-Hespériès (Paris, 1991); Gérard Sondag, *Le principe d'individuation* (Vrin: Paris, 1992); T. Barth, "Individualität und Allgemeinheit bei J. Duns Scotus," *Wissenschaft und Weisheit*, 18 (1955): 192-216.

[7] Scotus, *Tractatus*, 4.86: "In this first treatise I have tried to show how the metaphysical attributes affirmed of you can be inferred in some way by natural reason."

[8] For an analysis on the dating of the *Tractatus*, cf. the detailed introduction in Wolter, ix-xxiii.

access do we humans have to God? Scotus was philosophically intrigued with the way in which a finite human being could have access to some sort of inchoative knowledge of God. Today, scholars, and even some scientists, ask the same question: what access, no matter how one describes God, do human beings have as regards who or what "God" might be?

Over the many centuries of human existence, there have been several key positions on the manner in which one has access to God or to the transcendent. Although the following list generalizes these positions, it helps us understand the various ways that human beings in the past as well as in the present have understood how a human/God relationship can take place at all. The contemporary, highly visible term, "access," is deliberately used in the following pages. "Access" is a term that the computer age uses with abandon. It is even used today as a verb, namely: to access something. This term with its many implications speaks to the postmodern mind. Its use in such a statement as "how do we have access to knowledge of God and therefore to God's own being?" is far better than the medieval wording for the question, "how can we know God through the use of such terms as analogous, equivocal, and univocal?" Access to God has been, over many centuries, expressed in four different generalized scenarios:

A. The "God Has Spoken" Approach
B. The "Revelation of God in the Universe" Approach
C. The "Infused Knowledge" Approach
D. The "Natural Use of Human Reason" Approach

A. The "God Has Spoken" Approach

In this view, access to God is basically God accessing us. God reveals God's own self or a divine message. However, this revelation is not made directly to us, but only to special people: prophets, kings, emperors, holy saints, priests, popes, shamans, enlightened ones, etc. These people then relay to others what God has said. These "others" accept the message as coming from God, and their acceptance is a form of faith.

One might ask, however, what warrants such an acceptance of another's message about God? There have been several such warrants:

the holiness of the person; mysterious cosmic signs which all can see (e.g., earthquakes, eclipses, thunder and lightning, etc.); or miracles performed by the one who was granted the revelation. Even the threat of personal damnation has been used as a warrant.

The same is true in our Christian world. The Johannine gospel begins with the words: "The Logos became flesh and dwelt among us." This is an instance of God or Logos accessing us first, not we accessing God. Only when God or Logos accesses us, can Christians believe in Jesus who is both man and God. Others accept the Johannine statement, not because they have received a revelation from God, but, because of many complex factors, they have also come to accept this gospel as a revelatory statement from God. A standard Roman Catholic definition of faith, common throughout the twentieth century and learned by heart by many Catholics, expresses the same sentiment: "Faith is an assent by the mind to the truths revealed by God not because of their intrinsic evidence but because of the authority of God who revealed them." The magisterium of the Roman Catholic Church, as well as systematic theologians, have frequently designated a theological doctrine as *iure divino*, meaning that God, not the Church—*iure ecclesiastico*—has revealed this doctrine, and the doctrine consequently is immutable. Roman Catholics were instructed to accept such doctrine without any qualifications.

In the Jewish world of the Old Testament, the same pattern occured. God first accessed Abraham. Only then did Abraham and others follow God's instructions. This also happened with Noah, Jacob, Moses, and the prophets of Israel. God spoke to them and to other Old Testament figures as well. Their personal encounters with God and the messages they received from God were eventually described both in poetry and prose. Jeremiah offers reasons to accept a prophet's call: the fulfillment of the prophetic word (Jer. 28:9; 32:6-8); the prophet's fidelity to Jahweh and the religious traditions of Israel (23:13-32); the heroic witness of the prophet himself (1:4-6; 26:12-15.) Later in Old Testament times, these written accounts both of revelatory events and of the divine messages were codified in the Torah, the writings, and the prophets. Subsequently, centuries of Jewish people have believed in the written accounts of revelatory events and their divine messages.

The prophet Mohammed experienced similar revelations of Allah. These revelatory events and the divine messages they contained were written down in the sacred book, the Koran. Millions of people have placed their faith in these accounts of revelatory events and divine messages, even though they themselves have never had such a direct revelation of God in a way similar to Mohammed.

The "God has spoken to someone" approach assumes the validity of accepting the claim of someone that he or she has had a revelation of God. This approach has both strength and weakness. Its strength lies in the claim that "God" has spoken to a human person. The weakness lies in the veracity of such a claim, so that others might also accept "God's message." This same pattern of God accessing someone first and the warranting for acceptance of this claim by others can be found in almost all religious histories and cultures throughout human history. Naturally, each presentation has its own nuances and emphases. Still, the approach is based on God accessing someone first while the acceptance of such a revelation is secondary. Fundamentalism (Islamic, Christian, and Jewish) today presents strong similarities to this pattern. Fundamentalist leaders claim that their way of interpreting the revelation of God, as found in the Koran, New Testament, or Hebrew Scriptures, is the only way. They also claim that it is not their or anyone else's interpretation of the text that is compelling of acceptance, but the text itself, which is God's own word. Using many warrants for an acceptance of their interpretation, fundamentalist leaders have attracted followers who accept the leaders' interpretations as the exact textual readings. They do not acknowledge other interpretations since the text of God's word is clear in itself and is proclaimed without any hermeneutic.

As we shall see later, Scotus does not deny that God reveals God's own being to men and women. However, only if there is a basic and univocal relationship between God and human beings is the direct revelation of God intelligible to us. We shall see why Scotus makes this univocal proviso and why in his view it has a basic priority for any and all discussion on God's revelatory actions.

B. The "Revelation of God in the Universe" Approach

In this view the entire universe reflects God, the Creator, so access to God can be found in meditating on the world around us[9]. One

---

[9]Cf. Kenan Osborne, *Christian Sacraments in a Postmodern World* (Paulist Press: New York, 1999) chapter three, "Sacramental Structures in the World at Large," 54-83.

position in this approach regards particular cosmic events such as thunder and lightning, eclipses, comets etc. as the voice of God. The claim that these natural events are messages from God raises issues similar to those mentioned above. Who makes the claim that God is communicating to us in cosmic signs? And why should others accept such a claim? In the first way accessing God, God addresses a human being. In this second way of accessing God, God does not speak directly to a human being but speaks only through some cosmic event. Those who experience these cosmic events claim that these are signs from God. But can this claim be verified or validated in any way?

A more comprehensive approach, which some authors and scholars have presented, sees the entire universe as a reflection of God. These authors compare this reflection of God in the universe to a painting that is not signed but that can be appraised in much the same was as a painting by Degas, Chagall, or Caravaggio, an opera by Verdi or Wagner, or a symphony by Bach or Handel. If one is to find in the universe footprints of the creator God, one must have some prior inkling of what he or she is looking for. In the fine arts, a professional knows in advance something about Degas, Verdi, or Bach. Because of this expertise he or she can make a clear and acceptable judgment on whether the work is genuine or only an imitation. To assert that access to God can be found in God's "footprints" left in creation presupposes some factor or factors that allow a person to "find God."

In this regard also, our Franciscan tradition has something important to offer. Bonaventure employs exemplarism, i.e., God's exemplifying presence in all creation, together with illuminationism, i.e, illuminating grace that God has given us so that we can indeed recognize God's indirect appearance in nature.[10] Zachary Hayes offers a concise understanding of illumination in the writings of Bonaventure.

In the theory of illumination, the divine ideas function as a regulatory and motivating influence that illumines the human mind so that it is enabled to judge in accordance with the eternal truth. The ideas are not the direct object of human

---

[10]For Bonaventure, cf. Zachary Hayes, "Bonaventure: Mystery of the Triune God," *The History of Franciscan Theology*, ed. Kenan Osborne (The Franciscan Institute: St. Bonaventure, NY, 1994), 53-79; Francisco Blanco, *Imago Dei: Aproximación a la Antropología Teológica de San Buenaventura* (Editoriál Espigas: Murcia, 1993), 180-235.

knowledge, but are "constituted" obliquely, as it were, in the experience of finite beings.[11]

This position of Bonaventure on illumination is one of several such positions. It is fair to say that Bonaventure and Scotus are not at odds on this matter. Scotus would have no trouble with God enlightening the human mind with either "supernatural light," or "natural light," as Bonaventure teaches. Scotus asserts, however, that this manner of discourse is intelligible only if it is based on a primordial structure of reality, namely, the univocity of being. With this primordial and univocal structure of being, no other teaching on the relationship of God and the human person is possible. This will become clearer in the presentation of Scotus's view later in this essay.

Transcendental Thomism is similar. For example, Karl Rahner's analysis of the meaning of "being" allows him to speak of a supernatural existential. When or if "Being" (i.e. God) enters our world of discourse, the supernatural existential allows us to recognize the entry of divine Being itself, *Esse ipsum*.[12] The supernatural existential, which according to Rahner is part of human nature itself and not a supernatural gift of God, allows every human being to recognize the presence of God in this world at least in some inchoative way. The human intellect by its nature continually asks the question of being. When confronted with something that is not quite understood, the intellect asks: "What is it?" The same is true when and if God enters into the framework of our "being world." A person who does not recognize God in such a revelation can at least ask: "What is it?" In other words, if we see or hear something that we do not fully recognize, we can at least ask: "What is it?" To name anything "it" is a sign that a person already has some knowledge of "it."

On the other hand if we have no inchoative understanding of being, much less of God entering our "being world," or if we do not have the supernatural existential, we would not have a clue as to what we are looking for. The supernatural existential is an *a priori* that does not require or of itself lead to knowledge of God. Rather, if and when God accesses us, the supernatural existential, by its nature, allows a human

---

[11]Zachary Hayes, 92.
[12]Cf. K. Rahner, *Hearers of the Word*, Eng. trans. Michael Richards (Herder and Herder: New York, 1969) 31-44. The entire volume is a study on the *potentia obedientialis*, which Rahner later refers to as the supernatural existential.

being to recognize this divine accessing as an "it." From this tenuous "it" datum, one can then proceed to reflect on the further meaning of this "it," which means a reflection on God.

In many ways Rahner is correct in his claim that a revelation from God, an accessing of God, is meaningless, unless there is some sort of primordial relationship or at least some sort of philosophically possible relationship between the human construct and the "mode" of divine revelation. In his writings, however, it is clear that Rahner is speaking of something more profound than "mode." The human is a human being. A human being asks the question of being. Being is of the essence of the human construct and of the essence of all other beings of this world. Essentially, the philosophy of Rahner, and of many others, is a philosophy of being, and our entire universe is a "being world." When and if God enters into our "being world," God also enters as being, since God is essentially *esse ipsum*. If God were not *esse ipsum*, we would have no intelligible ability to recognize God in any form at all. God speaks to us in a "being framework." Rahner and others as well begin this line of thought with an unexpressed but essentially operative presupposition: God is *esse ipsum*, the Supreme Being. QED.

Not all human beings understand the world philosophically as a "being world." A philosophical being world is a Western way of philosophizing, stemming from Parmenides through Plato and Aristotle to Avicenna and Averroës; then, from Avicenna and Averroës to all the scholastics and from there to Descartes, Kant, Hegel, Husserl, Heidegger, and so on. Although a philosophy of being includes a very impressive group of thinkers, a majority of the human world does not have culturally such an all-pervasive philosophy of being. In fact, the wise men in these cultures have not and do not present an understanding of the world in terms of the Western philosophy of being. In another philosophical view God is not understood as *esse ipsum* or the Supreme Being. This is the reason why I have added *QED* to the position of Rahner et al.

Likewise, many theologians use analogy as a way to have access to God. Scotus does not discount analogy. Richard Cross summarizes the position of Scotus.

> Accepting the univocity theory does not commit Scotus to the claim that all theological statements are univocal. In fact, Scotus wants to defend the claim that most theological

statements are analogical. But he does not think that analogy is possible without univocity. I shall label the theories that Scotus opposes "non-univocity theories." Such theories defend the claim that *no* terms are applied to God and creatures univocally.[13]

Scotus himself says this very clearly: "Unless 'being' implies one univocal intention [i.e. concept] theology would simply perish."[14] Later in this essay I will indicate how primal being and the primal transcendentals of unity, truth, and goodness are for Scotus univocal. At this primal level Scotus considers all analogical discourse as equivocal, reducing all such analogical positions, including those of Thomas Aquinas and Henry of Ghent, to equivocation. A term is equivocal when it is used in two different and wholly unrelated senses. Scotus writes:

If you maintain that . . . the formal concept of what pertains to God is another notion, a disconcerting consequence ensues: namely that from the proper notion of anything found in creatures nothing at all can be inferred about God, for the notion of what is in each is wholly different.[15]

Authors who maintain that no terms are univocal when applied to God and creatures, such as Henry of Ghent and Thomas Aquinas, use either analogical concepts or equivocal concepts.[16] This position argues that if we humans see finite goodness or finite wisdom, we can infer that there is infinite goodness or infinite wisdom, because there is an analogy of proper proportionality between finite goodness and infinite goodness and between finite wisdom and infinite wisdom. Scotus argues that in all of these instances of analogy, exemplarity, and divine reflection, there needs to be some *a priori* inchoative understanding of what God is, whether this is called a form of illumination, a supernatural existential, or a supernatural readiness. Without this *a priori* inchoative understanding of God, one could not be led from the analogate to the

---

[13]Richard Cross, *Duns Scotus* (Oxford University Press: Oxford, 1999), 34, cf. also 147-148.
   [14]Scotus, *Lectura*, I.3.1.1-2, n. 113 (Vatican, 16: 266-267).
   [15]Scotus, *Ordinatio*, 1..3.1.1-2, n. 40 (Vatican, 3: 27).
   [16]For Henry of Ghent, *Summa Quaestionum Ordinarium* 21:2 c (Paris, 1520). For Thomas *Summa Theologiae* I:13.5 c.

primary analog. Scotus, of course, argues that this *apriori* inchoative understanding of God has to be univocal.

C. The "Infused Knowledge" Approach

Over many centuries some theologians have also spoken about a form of infused knowledge in human beings that allows persons to perceive, at least in some preliminary fashion, the presence of God.[17] Other theologians have spoken about a "natural desire for the supernatural."[18] In this approach for accessing God, there is some human *Vorverständnis* of what we are seeking. God provides us with a "natural desire" of the supernatural or with "infused knowledge" about God. The dialectical relationship of God to humans is another form of this access to God. Tillich's method of correlation is a good example of this.[19] In his *Systematic Theology*, Tillich clearly states that finite being asks the question of infinite being. Reason asks the question of God. History asks the question of eternal life. The human spirit asks the question of a Divine Spirit.[20] Schleiermacher's access to God is called *Das schlechthinnige Abhängigkeitsgefühl.*[21] Similarly, in Schelling's *Identitätsprinzip*, as expressed in Schelling III, there is *das unvordenkliche Sein*, an *Urgrund* open to the transcendent.[22] In the mystical writings of Böhme, there is also an *Urgrund* in which our human *Lebensgrund* and God's *Urgrund* coalesce in a mystical experience. Tillich speaks of a dialectical access to God. He states that when the thinking subject comes into contact with an object, the subject also comes indirectly into contact with the Ground of being, which is simultaneously one's own ground of being. "Das 'Itinerarium mentis ad rem' ist nur möglich als

---

[17]Theologians and religious leaders over many centuries and in most religions have claimed an infused knowledge from God or the transcendent. Gnosticism in the early Church claimed this inner enlightenment. In Christian theology since Alexander of Hales, a common position was that Jesus enjoyed a triple form knowledge: natural, infused, and beatific.

[18]Cf. Donald Gelpi, SJ, *The Gracing of Human Experience* (The Liturgical Press: Collegeville, MN, 2001), part one.

[19]Paul Tillich, *Systematic Theology*, vol. 1 (Chicago University Press: Chicago, 1965), 34-66. Cf. also K. Osborne, *New Being* (Martinus Nijhoff: The Hague, 1969), 84-145.

[20]Tillich, 41-46; Osborne, 3-8.

[21]F. Schleiermacher, *Der Christliche Glaube* (Walter de Gruyter: Berlin, 1984), Lehrsatz 14 and 15. Cf. K. Osborne, *New Being*, 63-69.

[22]Friedrich Wilhelm Schelling, *Philosophische Untersuchungen über der menschlichen Freiheit* (1809) (C. H. Beck: Munich, 1958). Schelling II is found in his writings from 1804 to 1813.

'Itinerarium mentis ad Deum.'"[23] In all of these authors there is some form of *Anknüpfungspunkt* or, as we might say in today's English, "access" to God.

The critique of these views of some sort of "infused knowledge" is based philosophically on the principle of a vicious circle. We know God because God has infused our minds with some sort of inchoative knowledge of God. The very goal of one's search is already present in some way when we begin the search. We already have gratuitously something of the very reward we are looking for.

D. The "Natural Use of Human Reason" Approach

I am not sure that it was necessary to provide such a lengthy description of the various possibilities of human access to God. Actually, it is in this fourth approach, using human reason alone, that I think Scotus's position clearly speaks to contemporary science, philosophy, and literature as regards the whole religious question today.

Scotus begins his philosophical approach to God by stating that everything that exists has a common factor. For Scotus this common factor is not God. He calls this common factor the "univocity of being." However, by "being" in this univocal sense he does not include in its content what the term "being" usually entails. Indeed, "univocal being" is almost contentless. Perhaps for our contemporary world, a better name for "univocal being" is a neologism, "isness." Scotus does not use the term "isness." I am using it to shelter the content of "univocal being" from all the profound ramifications of "being." Such a word, "isness," since it has no tradition, does not carry the baggage of meanings that the term "being" has. It is clear that the two terms are interrelated, but "isness" denotes and connotes only the least, the thinnest, and the slightest breath of being. The search for "isness" is similar to the scientific pursuit of the minutest particle in the microcosm. Is this particle matter or energy? Are neutrinos, which are so minute that they can be detected only indirectly, such a particle? Are microscopic photosynthetic bacteria the initial layers of life? Are these photosynthetic bacteria the basis, the *Urgrund*, for the entire organic world? Scientists struggle with these captivating researches. In a similar

---

[23]Tillich, "Kairos und Logos," *Gesammelte Werke*, vol. 4 (Evangelisches Verlagswerk: Stuttgart, 1961), 59.

vein, Scotus asks philosophically what is the primal base of every being, the *Urgrund* of being. He labels this *Urgrund* "univocal being," but I prefer to designate this metaphysical *Urgrund* as "isness."

There is an "isness" in every mineral, in every animal, in every person, and likewise, so Scotus says, in God. At first, however, he refrains from using the term God. Rather, he is searching for a first principle of all reality. This first principle is "isness." Similarly, for scientists today the neutrino may be the minutest piece of reality this side of nothingness, and the photosynthetic bacteria might be the minutest organic reality this side of all inorganic reality.

The opposite of "isness" is *absolute nothing*. In Greek this would be μηον ("not being at all") and not ουχον (a "not being here" but "being there," a "not being now" but a "being then"). "Isness" might be compared to a very thin tissue just this side of absolute nothingness. It is the sheerest web of positivity over against total negativity. In this sense, "isness" implies that if something is, its primal base is "isness."[24] If one asks the question whether God exists or not, Scotus states that such a search for God cannot even begin unless we ascribe "isness" to God or, better yet, to the first principle. "Isness" is the primal transcendental level of everything this side of absolute nothingness. Only on the primal basis of "isness" do all other forms of being ontologically have meaning and actuality.

Only after his analysis of the primal transcendental does Scotus consider the second level of transcendentals. There are three second-level transcendentals: the one, the true, and the good. Similar to the transcendental "one" is the transcendental number π, which includes all numbers from 1+ (to numerical infinity) and also from 1- (again to numerical infinity). The transcendental *one*, philosophically understood, includes all beings, which again are, in theory, numerically infinite.

The secondary-level transcendental, *one*, is metaphysically coterminous with "isness," the basic transcendental. For Scotus the opposite of this *one* is not two, three, etc., but nothing or metaphysical zero, absolute negativity. The unicity of "isness" is not at all similar to

---

[24]In the writings of Scotus, the question of univocal being is primarily focused on actual realty not mental realities. However, he does consider at times the status of *entia rationis*. Do these *entia rationis* also have "isness"? Is the primal being of purely mental constructs univocal being similar to the primal univocal being of actual being? This theme was debated in a more intense way among Scotistic scholars after Scotus himself died. It remains an unresolved issue.

the unicity found in more complex beings, e.g., all humans are of one nature. The unicity of "isness" is unique, since it is stating a unity of "isness" in every existent "isness," not just in some form of being, i.e., human nature. "Isness" and one are the same, but not quite a tautology.[25]

Similarly, "isness" is *true*. The opposite of true in this case is not false but absolute nothing. In ordinary discourse, not true or not real express negativity, e.g., this diary is *truly* written by Samuel Pepys; it is not *falsely* identified. People often claim that one statement is true while the other statement is false. Educators even employ true-false examinations, in which the students' answers are judged as either true or false. However, at the primal level of "isness," the opposite of true is not false but absolute negativity, just as the opposite of "isness" is absolute negativity. Primal "isness" and the second-level transcendental true are coterminous but not a tautology.

Similarly, "isness" is *good*. The opposite of the second-level transcendental good is not bad but absolute negativity. In ordinary discourse we speak of things that are bad and things that are good. Nonetheless, good things are metaphysically good *things*, and bad things are metaphysically bad *things*. In both instances "thingness" is positive not negative. Such a position in no way contravenes the onto-theological discussion of sin, which has a Christian tradition from Augustine to the present. In this long Christian tradition on the meaning of sin, sin is theologically presented as a *privatio* or a *carentia*, privation and lack. The "thingness" in bad things lacks some thing and is deprived of some thing. The "thingness" in bad things is not total and absolute "non-thingness," but the sinfulness of some thing or action is a non-being. No being or action is sinful in its positivity. It is sinful only in its negativity. At the level of "isness," however, the opposite of good is total negativity, not simply a *privatio* or a *carentia*. Similar to the second-level transcendentals one and true, *good* is coextensive with "isness" but the statement, "isness" is good, is not a tautology.

---

[25]To understand the relation of primal "isness" and primal one, Heidegger's volume, *Identität und Differenz*, in which he analyzes Parmenides's axiom, being is being, is philosophically very helpful. For Heidegger, the axiom, being is being, is not a tautology. There is an identity between the subject and the predicate but there is also a difference between the subject and the object. The delicate philosophical nuancing which Heidegger makes for Parmenides's axiom, being is being, is a valuable tool to understand Scotus's axiom, "isness" is one. This holds for his axioms, "isness" is true and "isness" is good.

In ordinary communication, these three transcendentals do not have the same meaning they have in Scotus's second-level transcendentals, which are co-extensive with primal "isness." In mathematics one speaks of such transcendentals as: sin x, log x and e^x. In philosophy one speaks of transcendental Thomism. In literature there are transcendental poets. In all of these instances, transcendental refers to given categories or series. When used with "isness," categories and series have no operative value. "Isness" transcends all categories and all series. One, true, and good likewise transcend all categories and series. Categories and series restrict the transcendentality of any and all categories and series. Primal "isness" and the second-level transcendentals, one, true, and good, transcend all categories and series. The second-level transcendentals, one, true, and good, are each univocally co-extensive with each other and with "isness." This is the position of Scotus.

The use of "isness," it might be pointed out, indicates that what Scotus means by the univocity of being is not at all a challenge to the analogy of being. The univocity of "isness" and the analogical use of being are in totally different spheres of discourse. Scotus, on the question of the first principle, rejects analogy not on the basis of univocity but on the basis of logic. How can one go from a finite analog to an infinite primal analog? Only at the level of "isness" can one and should one speak of univocity. At the level of primal "isness," analogical discourse is meaningless. At stages other than the primal stage and the second-level transcendental stage, e.g., polar transcendentals, analogical discourse is for Scotus a valid way of speaking.

At the third stage of transcendentals, Scotus begins to use a polarity of meaning. We can diagram Scotus's presentation of primal transcendentals as follows.

Third level: polarity

Second level: one, true, good

Primal level: "isness"

Transcendental polarity, for Scotus, means the polarity between past-future, right-left, temporal-eternal, finite-infinite, etc. Past-future can refer to many such polarities depending on the point of reference, for example, after the year 2000 or before the year 2000. Similarly, right-left can refer to many polarities depending on the point of reference, e.g., the right side of the mountain or the left side of the mountain, the right side of the river or the left side of the river. For Scotus, however, finite-infinite and temporal-eternal do not mean the same as the directional polarities. In the philosophical thought of Scotus, people encounter finite beings all the time. In these encounters one can ask: "If there are finite beings, is there infinite being?" Similarly, people encounter temporal beings all the time. In these encounters one can ask: "If there are temporal beings is there eternal being?" Even between these two polarities, finite-infinite and temporal-eternal, Scotus makes a distinction. It is not contrary to reason, he states, that there might be durational eternity or durational infinity. Scotus himself says that the universe around us might not have had a beginning nor might it have an ending.[26]

Today many scientists would say that the universe as we know it has no beginning and there is no indication that the universe will ever have an ending. The polarity, finite-infinite, excluding durational infinity, is quite different. Scotus indicates, however, that a durationally eternal universe is actually not infinite in the full sense of the term. For Scotus this involves a metaphysical distinction between an essentially ordered series and an accidentally ordered series.[27] The finite universe might be without beginning and without ending but even then the universe remains radically finite. At each stage in the evolutionary process there are limitations both for the microcosmic world and for the macrocosmic world. Infinity, however, implies non-limitation not only temporally but also in every other dimension of its being. A durationally infinite universe is basically an infinite, accidentally ordered series. However, such an accidentally ordered series is meaningless unless there is an essentially ordered series.

Faced with even the possibility of an accidentally ordered but durationally infinite evolutionary series, which cannot account for itself on the basis of *ex nihilo nihil fit*, the question still arises: Is there a first principle or a first agent? But can this question even be answered? It cannot be answered, Scotus argues, if there is absolutely no relationship

---

[26]Scotus, *Reportatio* 1.2.1.1-2, n.27; *Ordinatio* 1.2.1.1-2, n. 54 (Vatican Edition, 2:159-160). Cf. also Cross, 16-30.
[27]Scotus, *Tractatus* 3, 11.

between finite beings and an alleged infinite being. If there is no relationship, then a polarity in this transcendental, i.e., infinite being, exists only in the mind. Consequently, if one maintains that the finite universe, especially if there is durational infinity for this finite universe, has no need for any relationship to something outside of itself—here an alleged infinite being—then the finite universe is a self-sufficient reality. The presence today of our universe can be explained adequately by factors within the evolutionary system itself. Scientists have indeed found a richness of systems and interactions both in the microcosmic dimension and in the macrocosmic dimension. Finite and limited though these may be in themselves, experts in physics, chemistry, thermodynamics, biology, engineering, etc. find these systems and processes explanatory of almost all changes in the finite world. At times, new systems have been discovered, such as the Newtonian system or quantum physics. Scientists do not claim to have found or to have understood all such systems in our universe. To do so would contradict the openness of the universe as well as its randomness. Moreover, if one accepts the durational infinity of the finite universe, then there is no theory or valid doctrine of creation as many religious people profess. How does a supreme being create something that has no beginning and no end? Moreover, if there is no final end or parousia to the universe, then religious thought on the end time, the parousia or the rapture, would also need to be radically revised.

The apparent wandering off of the above paragraph is not at all irrelevant. Most Christian, Islamic, Hindu, and Jewish theologians explain the existence of an infinite being precisely through causation, both efficient and teleological. The scholars maintain that there is a fundamental relationship between the finite beings of our universe and the infinite being called God. This relationship is causal. But if there is neither beginning point nor end point to finite being, then the traditional arguments from efficient and final causality are called into question.

Although what has just been said is based on the possibility of durational infinity, and this itself cannot be proven, questions do arise. Why is there this systematized conglomeration of finite, contingent, and relational beings? Scotus again is helpful. For Scotus, nothing in this universe is necessary. Everything is contingent.[28] Nothing is absolute. Everything is relative. Nothing is infinite. Everything is finite. Nothing is intrinsically eternal. Everything is intrinsically temporal. Even in a durationally unending universe, there is no necessary internal agent that is the reason for the unending universe. An unending universe by itself is in its totality irrational, i.e., there is no reason (*ratio*) why it even is. A universe without beginning and ending is in its totality unnecessary, since even a complete summation of unnecessary finite beings does not in itself imply a necessity of the whole. A totally contingent universe even in its totality of contingent beings cannot as a totality be non-contingent. Specific systems within the microcosm or the macrocosm do have a relative necessity but only within their own systems. These systems "necessarily" act in some required fashion, but these systems are also contingent as is evident in the adaptation of life forms to new eco-systems and also the randomness found in both the microcosm and macrocosm. Contingent beings are changeable. The contingent systems formulated by physicists become antiquated and change whenever scientists find new aspects to upgrade or even cancel out these systems.

If everything in the universe is contingent, unnecessary, temporal, and finite, and there is no connection to an infinite, necessary, eternal being, then our universe is indeed irrational in its totality. Several postmodern philosophers have accepted primal absurdity.[29] In this scenario the question: Why is there a universe at all? is unanswerable. The universe is a theater of the absurd. The very question of God is to some degree irrelevant. Scotus, although allowing logically a durational infinity for the universe, does not concede that this infinite universe alone is self-explanatory. Durational infinity is only one series of philosophically infinite structures. Scotus calls these other foundational philosophical structures "essential orders." He writes:

What we intend to show from this is that an infinity of accidentally ordered causes is impossible, and that an infinity of essentially ordered causes is also impossible unless we admit a terminus in an essentially ordered series. Therefore there is no

---

[28]Cf. Vos Jaczn et al., *John Duns Scotus: Contingency and Freedom* (Kluwer Academic Publishers: Dordrecht, 1994).
    [29]Albert Camus, in his early writings, is typical of this acceptance of absurdity, and his novel, *The Stranger*, is an excellent literary presentation of a philosophy of the absurd.

way in which an infinity in essentially ordered causes is possible. And even if we deny the existence of an essential order, an infinity of causes is still impossible.[30]

According to Scotus, essential order is not a univocal term. Rather, it is an equivocal term, or as one might say today, it is a tensive term. Scotus states that in an essential order, nothing whatever is essentially ordered to itself.[31] An essential order is, as Wolter states, a disjunctive concept or construct.[32] For Scotus, there are two fundamental essential orders and three subdivisions of one of these essential orders. We can diagram this interrelationship as follows:

1. First Division of Essential Order   a. Eminence

                                              b. Dependence

2. Second Division of Essential Order   a. Causation

                                                 1.   Efficient

                                                 2.   Final

                                                 3.   Formal

                                                 4.   Material

                                              b. Gradated Conditionality

                                                 1.   Prius

                                                 2.   Postior

In all of the above, Scotus has used only a philosophical argumentation based on human reason alone. At the end of this section in the *Tractatus*, he has finally raised the issue of the reality of a first principle. Only when he infers on a philosophical basis the actuality of a first principle or first agent is this first principle named God. The relevance of Scotus's position today is seen in his strict use of human reason alone. No revelation, no infused knowledge, no footsteps in nature, no *Urgrund* of the human meeting the *Urgrund* of God, no

---

[30]Scotus, *Tractatus* 46. Cross, 16-30, indicates the weaknesses in some of Scotus's argumentation on the impossibility of an infinite, essentially ordered series.
[31]Cross, 14-15 and 174-175.
[32]Wolter, 174.

analogical presentation is included in his argument. In fact, from human reasoning alone, none of the above is a legitimate access to God. Only on the basis of primal "isness," second-level transcendentals (one, true, good), and third-level polar transcendentals—and these are all accountable only to human reason for their validity—is it possible to raise not a first principle question but the more difficult question, the God question. I believe that Scotus's presentation on a first principle speaks to a postmodern audience. If a postmodern audience can follow Scotus from primal "isness" to third-level polar transcendentals, then the further question, the God question, is at best a valid question.

To understand the Scotistic depth of this question of "isness" and "second level transcendentals," one needs to consider another major issue, namely Scotus's presentation of synchronic and diachronic contingency, which I also feel is a Scotistic and Franciscan position that speaks to a third millennium audience. There is moreover a third major issue that is needed for a full understanding of "isness" and the "second level transcendentals." This is Scotus's teaching on *haecceitas*, which also speaks to a third millennium audience. Generally, *haecceitas* is most vividly understood in its relationship to human beings. As Wolter once remarked in his explanation of *haecceitas*: "God did not create essences but individual persons."[33] In my view, *haecceitas* can be used in reference to the physical world. H_2O is abstract and generic, but the existent molecular structure is singular and individuated. *Haecceitas* can be applied in such a way that it involves our microcosmic structures and our macrocosmic structures. To do all of this however would make this essay far too long. Perhaps a second essay will be forthcoming.

---

[33]Wolter, *Duns Scotus' Early Oxford Lecture on Individuation* (Old Mission Santa Barbara: Santa Barbara, CA, 1992), xxvii.

Chapter Five

WHY PURSUE A DOCTORATE IN FRANCISCAN STUDIES TODAY?

Diane Tomkinson, O.S.F.

When Ilia Delio, O.S.F., invited me to speak on the topic of "Why Pursue a Doctorate in Franciscan Studies Today?" I naively thought preparing such a talk would be easy. After all, I have spent the past four years in Fordham University's Ph.D. program in historical theology, I am writing my dissertation on the Franciscan mystic Angela of Foligno, and I have plenty of opinions about the value of doctoral studies. However, as I started to write, I discovered that the meaning of the question was a little slippery, depending upon whom I imagined the audience to be. Am I speaking on behalf of those engaged in academics to justify our existence or appeal for support? Or am I addressing those outside the academy to invite them to the party? Do you need a doctoral degree to enjoy the banquet of the Franciscan intellectual tradition? Why would one pursue a doctorate in Franciscan studies? What AM I doing, why am I doing it, and why would I encourage anyone else to do it?

When we first spoke, Ilia suggested that a possible approach to my topic might be "the personal as paradigm." That is the direction my presentation will take. I am going to tell you the story of my conversion to doctoral studies. My own movement into such studies took part in two phases, which suggests a further division of our topic question. As the first phase, I will consider why one would pursue graduate, typically master's level, studies in Franciscanism. Secondly, I will consider why one would pursue such studies to the doctoral level.

In an essay on "The Intellectual Tradition in the Franciscan Order," Zachary Hayes, O.F.M., discusses Bonaventure's consideration of various motives for pursuing advanced study.[1] In the *Collations on the Gifts of the Holy Spirit*, Bonaventure follows Bernard of Clairvaux in

---

[1] Zachary Hayes, O.F.M., "The Intellectual Tradition in the Franciscan Order," *Ministrare Spiritum et Vitam: Congressus Repraesentantium Sedum Studiorum, O.F.M.*, Rome, July 4-13 1994; reprinted in *Franciscans Doing Theology*, ed. Mary C. Gurley, O.S.F. (St. Bonaventure, NY: The Franciscan Institute, St. Bonaventure University, 1999), 139-150.

identifying several inadequate reasons for pursuing advanced study, including idle curiosity, the desire for honors, and greed for monetary gain. (The last is probably not a very realistic temptation for most doctoral candidates in theology today.) Bonaventure agrees with Bernard that the two valid reasons to pursue knowledge are personal edification or spiritual growth, associated with the virtue of prudence, and the edification and instruction of others, described as charity.[2] I suggest that these remain fundamental reasons for pursuing advanced study in Franciscanism today. However, based upon my own experience, master's level study may be somewhat weighted toward the personal, while, because of the greater time, effort, and expense involved, doctoral studies may demand a deeper sense of mission.

I began my master's studies already blessed with a solid introduction to the Franciscan intellectual tradition in its various expressions from Francis and Clare to Bonaventure and Scotus. My initial formation as a Franciscan sister benefited from the outpouring of Franciscan scholarship in the eighties and nineties, as Franciscans pondered the eight hundredth anniversaries of Francis and Clare, the promulgation of the new Third Order Regular Rule, and the distinctiveness of the evangelical form of religious life. The sisters of my congregation who were responsible for initial and ongoing formation drew upon the work of well-known American Franciscan scholars, some of whom are represented in this collection of essays.

I was excited and fascinated by the spiritual and intellectual richness of the early Franciscan tradition. However, when I began my master's studies in 1992 at Washington Theological Union, my primary goal was to deepen my theological and liturgical knowledge and then return to pastoral ministry. My elective concentration in Franciscan Studies was motivated primarily by a desire for personal growth in the charism, although I did hope to share whatever I learned with my sisters. In Bonaventure's terms, my core courses were motivated by charity, and my Franciscan courses by prudence or personal growth.

However, the lines between the virtues of prudence and charity are not always easy to draw. During my studies, I was indeed edified by a deeper and broader encounter with the formative texts of the Franciscan tradition, further unfolding the theological depth in the apparent simplicity of the writings of Francis and Clare and the profound spiritual insight within the often frustratingly complex form of a writer such as John Duns Scotus. Yet I was also edified and sometimes perplexed by the resonances between the content of my Franciscan

---

[2]Hayes, "Intellectual Tradition," 141.

studies courses and many of the contemporary theological and pastoral questions addressed in my core classes. Were that many twentieth-century theologians really closet Franciscans?

My master's studies convinced me that our Franciscan intellectual tradition was rich with insights that could inform both contemporary theological speculation and contemporary pastoral practice. Why pursue graduate or master's level studies in Franciscanism? The simplest answer is because the Franciscan tradition is worth studying, retrieving, and living to the fullest extent possible. Graduate studies are one way to the deeper knowledge that allows us to integrate the Franciscan tradition more fully into all aspects of our lives and to pass it on as gift to others by word and example.

My master's level studies contributed to my growth both as a Franciscan and as a pastoral minister in the Church. I graduated looking forward to applying the full range of my studies to the challenges of pastoral ministry. Although some of my professors did urge me to consider doctoral studies, I resisted. I was perhaps overly sensitive to Francis's repeated warnings against a kind of knowledge that is rich in words and poor in deeds. As Admonition 7 warns: "Those religious are put to death by the letter who are not willing to follow the spirit of the divine letter, but, instead, wish only to know the words and to interpret them for others" (Adm 7:3).[3]

Desiring to follow "the spirit of the divine letter," I took my new degree and headed south. For three years I served as a pastoral administrator in a poor parish without a resident priest in rural South Carolina. I wanted the challenge of what seemed like a more radical Franciscan lifestyle, joining with other sisters to live among the poor and neglected and working with the people to identify and meet the needs of their community. At some deep level, without ever consciously articulating it, I assumed that Brother Giles was right—that too much time in Paris inevitably destroys the spirit of Assisi. Although I deeply respected my professors at Washington Theological Union, somewhere in my heart I still believed that the true Franciscan belonged among the *minores* of God's people—not among the books of the library. In effect, I exemplified that "reluctance to associate 'doing' with 'theology'" which Michael Blastic, O.F.M.Conv., laments.[4]

---

[3]"The Writings of Francis of Assisi," in *The Saint*, Vol. 1 of *Francis of Assisi: Early Documents*, ed. Regis J. Armstrong, O.F.M.Cap., J. A. Wayne Hellmann, O.F.M.Conv., William J. Short, O.F.M. (New York: New City Press, 1999), 132.
    [4]"The contemporary focus on ministry tends to dissociate being and doing from thinking, and there is a reluctance to associate 'doing' with 'theology.' It seems that we have dichotomized what for Francis and Clare and the founding Franciscan generations

Yet, in my parish ministry, I occasionally experienced the gift of sparking in others the excitement I had experienced myself during my studies: the excitement of reading a text, old or new, or listening to a speaker and suddenly being given the words that express or unpack or shed new light upon our lived experience. There is energy in discovering that Catholic theology is more than Thomas Aquinas, the Baltimore Catechism, or "Jesus loves you; draw a picture." (Choose your example depending upon your generation and your particular experience of Catholic catechesis!) There is a freedom in the recognition that the Church has a history and that things haven't always been the way they are today. I found some people in my small-town parish who were as hungry as Clare and her sisters were at San Damiano—hungry for good theology and good preaching, for the words, the images, the stories that helped them articulate and reflect upon the meaning of their lived Christian experience.

I found a similar hunger among the Franciscans I met in South Carolina, from both Third Order Regular and Secular communities. These present day sisters and brothers of the Poverello poured themselves out in often heroic ministries among the least of God's people. They were far from the workshops and symposiums of areas where there is a higher concentration of Franciscans. When the rare enrichment opportunity did arise, some of these sisters and brothers would drive for four or five hours to gather with other Franciscans to be nourished by input and reflection on our common tradition.

I began to learn in a deeper way how the Spirit that gives life, which Francis speaks of in Admonition 7, still lives in "the divine letter," not only in the words of Scripture but in the words of our Franciscan tradition—in the narrative theology of the stories of Francis and Clare, in the vernacular theology of their own writings, in the scholastic theology of Franciscan masters such as Bonaventure and Scotus, in the vernacular theology of mystics such as Angela of Foligno, and in the theological retrieval of these riches by contemporary scholars. The Spirit lives in such letters because these words continue to nourish the incarnate theology of contemporary Christians and contemporary Franciscans, even such as ourselves, who are the living words of this tradition. I would include among contemporary Franciscans both formal members of the three Franciscan Orders and all those who in some way

---

was an integral experience of Christian living." Michael Blastic, O.F.M.Conv., "'It Pleases Me That You Should Teach Sacred Theology': Franciscans Doing Theology," *Franciscan Studies*, 55 (1998): 1.

identify with the Franciscan tradition as a guiding force for their Christian life and mission.

In South Carolina, I began to discover that one could "do theology" gathered around a folding table in the parish hall or the kitchen table in the convent with ordinary Christians and ordinary Franciscans trying to make sense of their lives. And yet, the hunger around those tables could not be fed solely from local resources. Someone needed to do the work of gathering the ingredients of the Franciscan intellectual tradition, which is so thoroughly medieval in its origins, and making them accessible to the local tables of Christians on the brink of the twenty-first century. The possibility of learning more about the Franciscan tradition in order to sustain personal growth in the charism and a Franciscan sense of mission depended upon the scholarly efforts of those who further our knowledge of the tradition, "those who wish to know so that they may build up others; and this is charity."[5]

In their keynote addresses at national Franciscan gatherings in 1994 and 1995, Joseph Chinnici, O.F.M., and Zachary Hayes, O.F.M., eloquently articulated both the riches of the Franciscan intellectual tradition and its fundamental continuity from its beginnings in Francis and Clare through its more explicit theological articulations in the great Franciscan scholastics such as Bonaventure and Scotus.[6] They reminded the Franciscan family that this tradition was both our gift to cherish and our responsibility to pass on in response to the needs of the contemporary world. As part of this responsibility, Hayes and Chinnici called upon their listeners to begin to identify the next generation of Franciscan scholars. I heard of this verbal challenge from sisters of my own community who had been present at those gatherings and who invited me to see myself in the mirror of the words, "the next generation of Franciscan scholars." It was this call from my own sisters, especially those I admired for living the "life of Assisi" among the poor of South Carolina, which gave me the freedom to consider how I might

---

[5]Bonaventure, *Collations on the Gift of the Holy Spirit* (V, 478), quoted in Hayes, "Intellectual Tradition," 141.

[6]Although Chinnici's presentation focused on Franciscan evangelical life in the contemporary American context, he raised the question of retrieving "the Franciscan intellectual tradition of the mystics and theologians" as one of the ongoing challenges facing contemporary Franciscans; see Joseph Chinnici, O.F.M., "The Prophetic Heart: The Evangelical Form of Religious Life in the Contemporary United States," *The Cord*, 44.11 (Nov. 1994): 292-306, especially page 304. Hayes's presentation dealt explicitly with the Franciscan theological tradition; Zachary Hayes, O.F.M., "Christ, Word of God and Exemplar of Humanity: The Roots of Franciscan Christocentrism and Its Implications for Today," *The Cord*, 46.1 (1996): 3-17.

88 Diane Tomkinson

live the "life of Assisi," even in "Paris" (my metaphor for the contemporary academic setting).

As I began my doctoral studies at Fordham University, my experiences in South Carolina shaped my interest in the integral relationship between what has too often been considered separately as the spiritual and intellectual dimensions of the Franciscan tradition. How is the theological reflection of persons such as Francis, Clare, Angela of Foligno, and other Franciscan mystics related to the theological reflection of the scholastic theologians of the Order? Is the direction of influence only from Assisi to Paris, as Bonaventure and Scotus expand upon and articulate in scholastic language the insights of Francis and Clare? Or does the theology of Paris also shape the worldview of friars back in Italy? Does it trickle down, through them, to a lay, third order Franciscan such as Angela of Foligno, who repeatedly enters into animated theological discussions with her friar advisors and scribes about some of the most hotly disputed theological issues of the late thirteenth-century universities? Even more speculatively, does the theology of an Angela bubble back up, influencing the theology of the educated friars?

Scholars such as Bernard McGinn have begun to explore these mutual medieval influences under the categories of vernacular and scholastic theology,[7] but this question of the relationship between theology and spirituality, between our received tradition and our lived experiences, continues to be relevant today. Do those who have been shaped by the spiritual retrieval of the Franciscan charism over the past thirty years already know a kind of intuitive Franciscan theology, even if they can't put it into formal theological language? Contemporary liberation theologies, which do theology from the perspective of the *minores* of today in third world countries and among minority peoples in the United States, alert us anew to the danger of isolating Paris from Assisi. I think of a theologian such as Ada María Isasi-Díaz, who struggles to articulate a *mujerista* theology in which she serves not as the educated spokeswoman of her people, but as a facilitator empowering

[7]See McGinn's discussion of vernacular theology in the introduction to *The Flowering of Mysticism: Men and Women in the New Mysticism (1230-1350)*, Vol. 3, *The Presence of God: A History of Christian Mysticism* (New York: Crossroad Publishing Co., 1998), 19-30; and in his "Introduction: Meister Eckhart and the Beguines in the Context of Vernacular Theology" in *Meister Eckhart and the Beguine Mystics: Hadewijch of Brabant, Mechthild of Magdeburg, and Marguerite Porete*, ed. Bernard McGinn (New York: The Continuum Publishing Company, 1994), 1-14.

Hispanic women to speak in their own theological voice in a way that can be heard in the academy.[8]

Perhaps the charity Bonaventure speaks of is not only a matter of Franciscan scholars sharing their specialized knowledge of medieval and contemporary theological traditions with the rest of the Franciscan community or even with the larger world. What is the "charity" or the intellectual responsibility expected of those in daily contact with the wisdom of the poor and the wisdom of the everyday? How do we Franciscan academics stay in touch with the insights into the tradition that emerge around tables in the parish hall, the homeless shelter, the AIDS hospice, the school cafeteria, and the convent dining room? I don't know the answer to that question, but it seems to me an important one. If we are to be faithful to what we are learning about the culture of mutual exchange, which is part of our Franciscan intellectual tradition in its origins, then establishing such a culture today is also part of retrieving the tradition.

Although I desire to recognize a continuing "vernacular" or kitchen-table level expression of the Franciscan intellectual tradition, I do believe that there is an essential need for persons to continue to study this tradition at the doctoral level. Those gathered at the table in our kitchens, our parishes, our shelters, and our schools are not our only conversation partners. Part of the gift and the challenge of study at the doctoral level is that it brings us into new circles of conversation. To begin with, there is no institution in the United States where one can pursue a doctorate in Franciscan Studies per se. One gets a Ph.D. in the wider fields of theology, historical theology, history, or spirituality. Doctoral studies place the Franciscan intellectual tradition into these wider contexts. This is not only an academically but a spiritually appropriate approach to our tradition and charism. Thirteenth-century Franciscans "did theology," which acknowledged and responded to the changing spiritual, ecclesial, economic, political, and ecological contexts of their world. The world was their cloister and their conversation partners were many. Can we do any less?

Franciscan scholarship at the doctoral level strives to name what is distinctively Franciscan about a tradition that is so deeply immersed in and shaped by the concerns common to its larger world, in both the thirteenth and the twenty-first centuries. As one medieval history professor challenged me: "If all you ever read are Franciscans, how do you know what is unique and distinctive about what the Franciscans

---

[8]See Ida María Isasi-Díaz, *Mujerista Theology: A Theology for the Twenty-first Century* (Maryknoll, NY: Orbis Books, 1996), 1-9.

have to say?" Much that we tend to claim as Franciscan was originally
part of a wider twelfth- and thirteenth-century conversation.
Franciscans did not invent the idea of *imitatio Christi*. The penitential
movement, the theological and philosophical tradition that prioritized
the good over being and devotion to the humanity of Christ all predated
the Franciscans. Francis, Clare, and their followers gave flesh to these
ideas and developed them in ways we can identify as distinctively
Franciscan, but only if we are willing to admit that thirteenth-century
Franciscans were already part of a conversation which was older and
larger than they.

How do Franciscans in the twenty-first century continue to be part
of conversations larger than ourselves? One of the risks of the strong
sense of intra-Franciscan sisterhood and brotherhood shared by those of
us who are members of the three Franciscan orders is that we can be
satisfied just talking with one another. And yet we are inescapably part
of a larger Church and world. These have already shaped our
conversation and need us to contribute to their ongoing discourse.
Doctoral studies have made me more aware of how both our scholarly
retrievals and our popular reception of the Franciscan tradition have
been and continue to be shaped not only by the theological conversations of the thirteenth century but also by the theological and
historiographical conversations of our own time. The questions we ask
of the tradition arise out of our experience of our own changing world.
One example is the dialogue between theology and the sciences, to
which Ilia Delio and Zachary Hayes have referred. Another is the
growing body of research exploring the contribution of Clare and other
Franciscan women to the origins and subsequent development of the
Franciscan tradition, including its intellectual dimension. This research
has been influenced by the questions and methods of late twentieth-
century feminist scholarship. The retrieval of the tradition does not
occur in a vacuum.

The contemporary retrieval of the Franciscan intellectual tradition
is influenced not only by contemporary events and current topics of
conversation but also by an expanding circle of conversation partners.
We ask: "Who will carry forward this Franciscan intellectual tradition?"
We now realize that, most likely, it will not be only or even primarily
members of the three recognized Franciscan orders. Some of the most
significant new work in Franciscan studies is being done by lay scholars,
both in Europe and in this country, and by religious from other
congregations who study Franciscan figures. These scholars often ask
different questions and come up with different readings than those we
have taken for granted within the Franciscan family. Such new insights

may be some of the new influences which Ilia Delio suggested are needed for "new patterns of order" to emerge in a dissipating system.[9] The three orders are stewards of the Franciscan intellectual tradition, but we are not its sole proprietors. How do those of us formally identified as members of the Franciscan family collaborate with this new generation of lay scholars? How do we invite them into our circle of conversation? Why aren't more of them here today?

The opportunity to converse with such peers, both those who study the Franciscan tradition and those who focus on contemporary theological issues, remains one of the most exciting aspects of my doctoral studies. These conversations further convince me that our tradition does have something to offer to the contemporary theological enterprise. The women in my dissertation peer group are working on topics ranging from ecological theology to a relational ecclesiology to a feminist retrieval of the *agape* tradition of God as Love. I am constantly excited about the resonances between their work and the Franciscan intellectual tradition. In my own dissertation research, I hope to retrieve the Trinitarian theology of Angela of Foligno as a vernacular expression of the Franciscan theological tradition. This may serve as a resource for contemporary feminist theologians whose efforts in the area of Trinitarian theology have thus far primarily engaged the Cappodocian and Thomistic traditions.[10]

My friends at Fordham tease me about being a shameless proselytizer for the Franciscan intellectual tradition. I am increasingly aware of the need to bring the "minor voice" of our Franciscan theological tradition into the conversations of contemporary theologians who are neither Franciscan nor particularly interested in things Franciscan. Those of us, whether religious or lay, who do study the Franciscan intellectual tradition, repeatedly express our conviction that it has great resources to offer to the burning issues of contemporary theology. How do we make these resources more available and attractive to the larger academy? How does the broader Franciscan family support its scholars, both religious and lay, in such an effort, which is a form of Franciscan mission?

All of these questions, issues, and possible contributions are my reasons for pursuing doctoral studies related to the Franciscan tradition.

---

[9]See Delio's article in this book, "The Franciscan Intellectual Tradition: Contemporary Concerns," pp. 1-19.
[10]Significant feminist efforts in Trinitarian theology include Catherine Mowry LaCugna's *God for Us: The Trinity and Christian Life* (San Francisco: HarperSanFrancisco, 1991) and Elizabeth Johnson's *She Who Is: The Mystery of God in Feminist Theological Discourse* (New York: Crossroad, 1992).

They are the reasons I would encourage others to pursue and/or support such scholarship. After eight hundred years, the Franciscan intellectual tradition is still fruitful. The Spirit still needs harvesters to bring this fruit to those who sit at the tables of the academy, the parish, the shelter, the classroom, the boardroom, and the community room. Such a pursuit of knowledge remains the ministry of charity that Bonaventure affirmed.

Doctoral studies, of course, also have their "prudential" dimension, which constitutes a possible source of personal spiritual growth. The Franciscan tradition has always insisted that theology is a practical science, ultimately oriented toward the knowledge that is loving union with God. One of my favorite descriptions of the personal impact of doctoral studies is that it expands the boundaries of one's ignorance. I graduated from Washington Theological Union thinking that I had learned quite a lot about theology. I approach the attainment of my Ph.D. knowing that what I have learned is just a tiny sliver of all there is out there to know. This recognition of our intellectual limits is also part of a Franciscan wisdom tradition that reverences the mysterious depths both of God and of every creature in its individual "thisness." Personal Mystery is never fully known. As Angela of Foligno taught her conversation partners in doing Franciscan theology, the joy of beatific union with the Trinity will be a "joy of incomprehension; [the saints] understand that they are not able to understand."[11]

---

[11]Angela of Foligno, "Instruction 3," in *Angela of Foligno: Complete Works*, trans. & intro. Paul Lachance, O.F.M., pref. Romana Guarnieri (Mahwah, NJ: Paulist Press, 1993), 239.

Chapter Six

JOHN DUNS SCOTUS: RETRIEVING A MEDIEVAL THINKER FOR CONTEMPORARY THEOLOGY

Mary Beth Ingham, C.S.J.

In his short monograph on Thomas Aquinas,[1] Anthony Kenny noted that the value of this thirteenth-century Dominican lay not so much in the answers he offered for certain questions, but rather in the questions he raised and the way in which he raised them. Today, I would like to make something of the same argument for John Duns Scotus. As you consider the value of your own spiritual and intellectual tradition, I suggest that you look at Scotus not so much for original and new answers to contemporary questions (although there are certainly original insights in Scotus, as I will note later), but rather for the manner in which Scotus viewed all that exists.

As the third millennium opens before us, it is important to recognize the way in which contemporary reflection (whether philosophical or theological) recognizes its limits and searches for another model or paradigm. The cold war is over. Modern thought has been superceded by the so-called post-modern. Models of scientific objectivity and rationality no longer appear to help us deal with contemporary issues. Spiritual yearnings express themselves in New Age religion. In addition, the post-renaissance notion of science has done violence to creation. Technology dominates our societies, threatening human dignity and values. The world's goods are not shared equally; indeed the gap between rich and poor widens. In short, we are at a global turning point. We cast about for other ways of seeing our reality, hoping to find a way to integrate a world that has become too complex, too fragmented for us to bear.

Medieval thinkers hold a key for us today. I do not mean that we must return to a time in history that is long gone. Rather, I think that

---

[1]Past Masters Series, Cambridge University Press.

by taking a closer look at their intellectual legacy we might discover principles to help us integrate the scientific with the religious, the intellectual with the spiritual. We do not need to return to a triumphalist notion of religion to take advantage of the legacy of medieval thinkers. They can help us *precisely* insofar as they were religious and spiritual thinkers who saw the world in which they lived as a coherent whole. Therefore, the value of a person like Scotus today stems from his Franciscan vision of reality, as he articulates his intellectual insights to form a coherent whole where scientific, intellectual, and spiritual values are all present. In other words, the coherence of Scotus's intellectual insights (both philosophical and theological) stem from his spiritual vision, *precisely* insofar as he is a Franciscan.

My paper serves, then, both as an example of the contemporary relevance of the Franciscan intellectual tradition and a call to you to continue that tradition today in your own reflection on contemporary issues. This you must do from the perspective of your religious and spiritual heritage. If you hold (as I think you would) that the insights of Francis of Assisi are relevant today and that the Franciscan life has a witness for our world, then you must conclude that the intellectual formulation of those insights can be a powerful influence at a time in history when we need new intellectual models, new conceptual paradigms to understand our place in the world, our relationship to God and to one another, and ways that we might promote the Reign of God in our own day.

In my own case, Scotus offered a series of interesting philosophical insights until I recognized the spiritual point behind it all. I had struggled for years to make sense of it and then, one day, it all fell into place. That was the day I realized the centrality of beauty for him as a Franciscan, along with the role of love and creativity. Creativity, love, and beauty are the foundation of his intellectual vision because of the particular spiritual tradition to which he belongs. I find that where scholars misread or misunderstand Scotus they have not taken adequate account of his spiritual vision precisely as a Franciscan. This vision is grounded in the power of ordered loving as central to a correct understanding of human nature as rational, on the Trinity as model both for reality and for human relationships, and on an aesthetic perspective that is the basis for his discussion of moral goodness.

I have come to the conclusion that Scotus's philosophical insights cannot easily be separated from his theological pre-occupation, nor should they be. Here is a thinker who is consciously spiritual in his intellectual endeavor, consciously Christian in his understanding of the divine nature, without dismissing the value of insights that come from other non-Christian perspectives. The God of Scotus is the God of John 3:16, who so loved the world he gave his only Son. He is the God of Paul's letter to the Ephesians 1: 4-6, who predestines all to glory. He is the God of Matthew 20, the Master who rewards workers far beyond what they deserve and wonders why some grumble because he is generous. Here is a notion of divine justice interpreted in terms of divine mercy and liberality, not in terms of a strict understanding of giving what is due. The God of Scotus is the God of Francis, a God so generous he throws everything away out of love. This may be the very God our world so needs today.

I think there has always been a tension within the Franciscan tradition between the intellectual and the spiritual. With his concept of rationality as ordered loving, Scotus offers a way in which we might understand this tension as creative, insofar as it offers a renewed and more integrated way to understand the human person as both scientist and artist, philosopher and poet, a person of rational faith. In this he escapes the pitfall of Thomism, which more consciously embraces the scientific and philosophical. For Scotus, the aesthetic is more basic than the scientific and intellect is integrated within a broader context, defined not by knowing but by loving.

Generosity and love constitute the basis for Scotus's discussion of the Incarnation. With him, we enter a Christocentric vision of salvation, considered independently of human sinfulness. Our categories of soteriology must change from those of justice to those of generosity. More importantly, we must focus on the divine desire to be present with us. This approach must have pastoral implications. Divine delight becomes a category within which we consider creation and the value of each being as pleasing to God (a metaphysical consideration). Within this category of divine delight, we understand the motivation behind the covenant, both with the People of Israel and in the Incarnation (a theological insight). From this category, finally, we anticipate the glory that awaits us and how we might participate in divine life by imitating divine creativity (the moral perspective).

It is against the larger framework of divine delight that I consider more carefully, in what follows, three aspects of Scotist thought in order to bring out how each integrates the intellectual with the spiritual in a vision framed by love. The most basic insight that Scotus presents about God is that the Trinity delights in itself, in the created order that reveals such beauty, and in the human heart that seeks to realize beauty in each of its choices. A vision of aesthetic delight—this is what Scotus offers us today.

If we begin with the assumption that Scotus is valuable precisely insofar as he elaborates Franciscan intellectual and spiritual insights, then we can organize these insights spiritually around the importance of creation, the centrality of the covenant, and the goal of communion with one another and with God in love. In this way, we might understand Scotus's contribution to contemporary reflection in both horizontal and vertical dimensions.

The Value of the Created Order

For those of us outside the Franciscan spiritual tradition, no aspect appears more central to Franciscan spirituality than that expressed by Francis in the *Canticle to the Sun*. In affirming the value of creation and our relationship to it, we affirm the value of the contingent, the ephemeral. Affirming this value, we recognize the beauty of the present moment as it expresses the perfection of the eternal. In other words, the recognition of the value of the contingent—the realm that does not have to exist or that could be other than it is—involves the affirmation of the value of divine desire and creative choice. God's choice to create this world, the one that surrounds us, is understood as a single choice that involved many (possibly an infinite number of) options. And yet, our world was chosen and created. One does not have to conclude that we are "the best world possible," but one would be foolish not to see in this the enormous love and delight of the Creator for the created. Since God is not only the source for creation, but also the Sustainer of all that is, the actual and present existence of what exists gives testimony of the ever-present and sustaining love of God for what has been made. God did not have to create in order to be God. Nothing about the divine essence required such generosity. The only thing required by the divine essence was that, if God did choose to create, God must remain God.

A second aspect revealed by the importance of the contingency of the created order is seen in the better-known Scotist affirmation of the primacy of each individual. Here is that *haecceitas*,[2] the "thisness" so dear to the poet Gerard Manley Hopkins. As created by God, each being is a "this," a *haec*, incapable of cloning or repetition, the ultimate reality of being, known fully to God alone. No human person is reducible to physical characteristics, genetic makeup, or DNA. The sacredness of each person, indeed of each being is philosophically expressed in this term *haecceitas*. The created order is not a transparent medium through which divine light shines, but is itself endowed with an inner light that shines forth from within.

Finally, the dignity of the human person is expressed by Scotus in the natural powers of cognition and human rationality. We are not created independently of the natural order. Our powers of cognition and rationality are perfectly adjusted to the way the world is, because both the faculties of human reason and the ordered whole of creation are the result of the divine creative act. Unlike Aquinas, who speaks of only mediated access to the world around us, Scotus balances in his theory of knowledge both mediated and immediate access.[3] His understanding of the requirements for the beatific vision necessitates a cognitional theory that already equips human reason with all that it needs to see God face to face. Thus, in addition to the abstractive knowledge that Aquinas refers to, Scotus adds that human reason possesses an intuitive cognition of the world. This immediate cognition is not what we mean by "intuition," but points to an immediate existential grasp of any existing reality in its existence.

As Scotus works out his explanation for this more immediate ability, he offers two reasons, both based on the dignity of the human. In the first place, it was part of Christ's rational grasp of the world around him and of the presence of his Father. In his humanity, Jesus mirrors our own human potential. In the second place, such a capacity is absolutely necessary for our experience of the beatific vision. In other words, if we are able to see God face to face, then our rational constitution must have what it takes and by nature. Scotus sees no need for the "light of glory" that Aquinas provides in order for the beatific vision to take

---

[2]The Latin term only appears twice in Scotus's works, in the *Reportatio* II, distinction 3 and in his *Subtle Questions on Aristotle's Metaphysics*, VII, q. 13.
[3]In *Ordinatio* II, d. 3, q. 2.

place. It belongs to human dignity, as currently created by God, to
enjoy the relationship of communion that awaits us at the end of this
life. Certainly, our ability to enjoy all aspects of our rational
constitution has been limited by the consequences of original sin, but
this does not mean such rational powers do not belong to us by nature.[4]

The Centrality of the Covenant

Scotist thought offers a beautiful integration of biblical and
doctrinal insights. At the foundation of his reflection upon God's
relationship to the world and to us is the notion of the covenant
initiated by God and fulfilled through the Incarnation. Salvation history
is the large lens through which Scotus looks at what it means to be
human: the call of Abraham, the revelation to Moses, the Exodus, the
centrality of Christ, and predestination of all to glory. Here are the
signposts of his thought.

In his Prologue to the *De Primo Principio* (Scotus's argument for
God's existence), he sets up the discussion with an allusion to the
theophany of the burning bush and God's revelation to Moses as "I am
who am." It is only within the framework of divine self-revelation as
being that human reason is able to reflect upon and conclude to the
existence of an infinite being, foundation for the natural order. In this
"Metaphysics of Exodus," Scotus integrates the central tenets of the
Judeo-Christian tradition with the best of philosophical speculation on
the nature of existence and its rational requirements. He also affirms the
importance of language about God. Since God has revealed himself as
being, human reason can speak about God in an authentic manner. The
divine is not mystery beyond reason or beyond our ability to
communicate what we experience of God. Paradoxically, God lies both
beyond and within our ability to express our spiritual intuitions as
accurately as we are able. Thus theology does not replace spirituality,
but gives formal expression to a lived experience.

Perhaps the most original aspect of Scotist thought is his rejection
of Anselm's argument for the Incarnation found in the *Cur Deus Homo?*
When he considers the reason behind the Incarnation, Scotus affirms
quite clearly that God would have become human *even if* Adam and Eve

---

[4]See, for example, his discussion in *Quodlibet* 14, n. 12.

had not sinned.[5] Thus, the Incarnation is not a divine response to human sin. Sin is not the center of our consideration of the covenant. If it were, he states, then we would rejoice at the misfortune of another (the *felix culpa* argument). Rather, the Incarnation expresses the fullest communion of God-with-us. It is not sin, but Christ who is the center of our attention. This is not to deny sin or human weakness, but it is an important change of focus for both philosophers and theologians. As we move into a new millennium, we are in need of a renewed anthropology—a renewed vision of what it means to be human. Scotus may offer the most fruitful medieval path in this reflection, for he consciously rejects a soteriology that is founded upon a negative anthropology.

If the Incarnation took place as an event in history, not because of human sinfulness nor out of a need for divine retribution but as the manifestation of divine desire to be with us, then what might *salvation* really mean? How might this understanding of divine desire inform our missionary attitudes toward other cultures? How might it transform our ecumenical approach to other religious traditions? Perhaps salvation involves neither justification nor retribution, but is the simple act of *presence*. If this is the case, then the celebration of Eucharist takes on a renewed meaning as a salvific act.

The notion of covenant grounds, finally, Scotus's understanding of moral living as relational living. In the revelation of the law to Moses we find both the articulation of the demands of the covenant and the basis for any social fabric. The moral foundation represented by the Decalogue reveals the primacy of relational living for Scotus. His is not primarily a divine command theory. The ten commandments reveal God's desire for us and point to the best way we can show our love for Him.[6] Our relationship with God and with one another is strengthened by our choice to follow out of love what God asks of us. But the law is not the final word and Scotus is not a legalistic thinker. For him, love for God is the only unconditionally binding commandment.

Moral living is also relational living within the human heart, where the two natural affections (for justice and for happiness) come together in the desire to love God above all things. Thus, moral goodness involves both a social dimension and an internal, spiritual experience of

---

[5]In *Ordinatio* III, d. 7, q. 3.
[6]In *Ordinatio* III, 37, unica, n. 12.

harmony and integration. The joy and delight experienced by the good person reveals that the deepest human longing is fulfilled by right and ordered loving. This perfects our nature as rational beings made in God's image.

The Insight about Communion

Finally, the relationship realized in the covenant contains a revelation about God as Triune relationship and as ground for the entire moral order. This is Scotus's way of expressing the key insight that "God is love." This truth expresses both the nature of God and grounds all choice. As Scotus states: "God is to be loved" is the foundational principle for all action, human as well as divine. His focus on the human will (or his voluntarist approach) is really a focus on the power of love, the perfection of which reveals the fullest understanding of the human person as rational and as created in the image of God.

Here is, for me, the most important aspect of an accurate retrieval of Scotist thought. Our contemporary notions of rationality are framed by modern philosophy, by the intellectual revolution of post-Cartesian and Kantian philosophy. This revolution currently frames the questions that can be asked. It names the thinkers who are worth reading, the thoughts worth thinking, the topics worth pursuing. Today, rationality means the ability to think, to solve problems, to get the right answers, to get the result we desire. Rationality is tied to calculation, such that one wonders if computers are human since they can reason as we do and indeed even faster that we can!

The question of artificial intelligence as rational would amuse someone like Scotus, because his notion of rationality is much broader than the ability to analyze. He ties it to love and the human ability to choose to love the highest good, to be capable of self-control. Rationality has nothing to do with the human intellect, since this is merely a tool that serves in deliberation. Scotus's approach to the question of rationality begins with the will, that is, the human affective desire for union with God. If the fullest development of the rational person involves love and communion, then the ability to think rightly is only a small part of a much larger picture of what it means to be human.

In his Commentary on the Questions of Aristotle's *Metaphysics*, Scotus states quite clearly that the intellect is only rational when it works with the will, that is, when it is informed by and serves the activity of ordered loving. It is so easy, he explains, to confuse the intellect with rationality, since at the first turn to introspection, we are distracted by the activity of intellectual reflection.[7] This is what happened to Aristotle, and (he might add) to most philosophers. But one must reflect more deeply on one's experience to discover that it is not the intellect at all, but the will (seat of love) that holds the key to rational perfection. The will's natural internal constitution defines rationality. There are within the will two distinct metaphysical orientations: the first, directed toward its own preservation and well-being; the second, directed toward the highest good.[8] Both orientations come together in God in a two-fold manner. First, in God alone do we find that being for whom love for the highest good is, in fact, identical to love for the self. Thus, every act of God reveals the unity of the divine essence and holds out the goal of rational perfection. In human moral development, we strive to unite the two moral affections (as he calls them) and bring love for the self into harmony with love for the good. When we do this, we imitate divine goodness and simplicity. When we do not, we are simply not ourselves. This is what it means to sin. I once heard a priest say that the best way to begin a confession would be simply to admit: "I haven't been myself." How wonderful it would be, in pastoral settings, if we could simply ask: "Have you been yourself?"

Finally, an aspect that comes out of a closer focus on love is the role of beauty as moral category and as a way of integrating the human moral journey into the spiritual journey. A moral aesthetic is, I think, quite Franciscan and could prove to be extremely timely for contemporary reflection. The focus on beauty in Scotist thought brings together divine and human orders of love. In human moral choices, we seek to love the good. Scotus describes the morally good act as a beautiful whole,[9] a work of art in which all dimensions are in harmony. This act and the morally good person are made even more beautiful by the presence of charity. Here Scotus moves from the order of moral goodness to the order of merit—a move from nature to grace, from philosophical to theological domains. In the order of merit, the divine

---

[7]See Book IX, question 15, n. 7.
[8]In *Ordinatio* II, d. 6, q. 2, n. 8.
[9]In *Ordinatio* I, d. 17, q. 2, n. 62.

ear delights in the music of human goodness informed by love. The good act informed by charity stands at the boundary between the realm of human freedom and love and the realm of divine freedom and generosity. This is the entrance to deeper relationship made possible by divine *acceptatio*, where God chooses freely to reward human actions far beyond what they deserve according to a strict justice.[10]

Scotus's use of an aesthetic approach to explain his moral insights has significance today in light of three key aspects. First, an aesthetic model addresses and integrates the intricacy at the heart of the virtue vs. principle moral dynamic. Learned behavior does indeed form character. Principles offer a coherent and integrated whole for the morally mature agent. The domain of human *praxis* includes internal and external realms of intention and performance that are not in opposition. Together they form that harmonious unity of character called integrity.

Second, the artistic imagery used by Scotus throughout his texts (moral and metaphysical) supports the focus on love and beauty, both in human moral choice and in the order of divine *acceptatio*. The native freedom of the human will moves toward the good and seeks to love in an ordered and appropriate manner. The affection for justice finds its object in the *bonum honestum*, or the good of value. For Alexander of Hales, *bonum honestum* was synonymous with intelligible beauty.[11]

Third, the artistic imagery integrates the notion of *praxis* around the functioning moral agent. Like the artist or musician, the moral person follows a high standard. Yet the acts of the moral expert are not different in kind from those of any moral agent. Proper and appropriate moral decision-making is the goal of human agents. The moral expert, like the trained artist, is able to do better and more quickly what we all strive to do. It is not simply a question of choosing, but of choosing well, "rejoicing, loving and hating rightly."[12]

The aesthetic preference in Scotus reveals, additionally, his connection to the twelfth-century monastic spiritual tradition, with its development of the Patristic insights around moral wisdom and discernment. In speaking of the notion of practical wisdom, we often

---

[10]In *Ordinatio* I, d. 17, q. 1, n. 149.
[11]"Cum bonum dicatur dupliciter, honestum et utile. . . . Honestatem autem voco intelligibilem pulchritudinem." *Summa Theologica* I, n. 103; I: 162. Taken from Allan B. Wolter, *The Transcendentals and their Function in the Metaphysics of Duns Scotus* (St. Bonaventure, NY: The Franciscan Institute, 1946), 100, note 1.
[12]Aristotle, *Politics*, 1340a 15.

use the term prudence. In the Middle Ages, this term had two traditions: the Stoic/Patristic and the Aristotelian. In the Stoic/Patristic tradition, prudence was one of the cardinal virtues, tied either to temperance (as in Ambrose) or to justice (as in Augustine). Scotus's own treatment of prudence recalls the twelfth-century wisdom tradition of monastic spirituality. He describes the prudent person as one who "sees" the moral situation in a particular way, one who has a different perspective, almost a divine perspective. There is very little work being done on the connection between the spiritual tradition of the twelfth century and what was happening with men like Aquinas and Scotus in the thirteenth century, as they developed the new philosophy of Aristotle. It is clear that these men wrote what they wrote against a context that was well formed. They were members of religious orders whose spiritual vision formed their own. This vision finds few representatives today within the larger academic and scholarly community. Who better to represent such a vision than women and men for whom it is a living tradition?

I am increasingly convinced that much of the "language" Scotus speaks is spiritual and religious. A contemporary scholar with no sense of the Franciscan vision cannot hope to understand what is really going on behind his arguments. If those of us who live within the tradition of religious life or within Franciscan life in particular do not enter the conversation at the scholarly level, we cannot blame our colleagues for missing the point. It is up to us to find ways to make the spiritual argument an integral part of the larger scholarly and intellectual argument. But this is really to say it is up to us to participate in the birthing of a new vision of the human: one where the spiritual and rational are better integrated.

Closing Reflections

In closing, I would like to point to several specific areas where more study in Scotus would be beneficial. The aesthetic dimension is clearly undeveloped, both in terms of its sources in the Franciscan tradition and its implications for the moral-spiritual-pastoral. This is an area that Thomas does not develop, so it would be fairly simple to develop something independently of how a Thomist would view the matter.

In addition, I suspect that there may be Stoic influences present in Scotus and in his moral presentation of prudence and moral discernment. These Stoic patterns would have clearly been developed through Augustine, Ambrose, and the monastic writers. Literally nothing exists on this, to the best of my knowledge.

The notion of moral discernment points to a possible alternative model for moral decision-making, neither consequentialist nor Kantian. This might represent the most original contribution of the Franciscan tradition, especially as it could bring together scholars of several seemingly opposed traditions around a common theme, thereby promoting peace in the academic community.

As a non-Franciscan and, indeed, a non-theologian, I hope my reflections have helped to shed some light on a serious consideration of the rightful place of Franciscans in the scholarly community and on the enormous intellectual legacy men like Duns Scotus have left behind. They may speak the Franciscan spiritual insights in a technical language that Franciscans may not recognize as theirs today, but their words are every bit as faithful to the spirit of Francis as any poetry or music. They exalt the dignity of the human person, the centrality of Christ and the Incarnation, the enormous generosity of a God who has richly provided for all his children. Franciscans enjoy an aesthetic spiritual tradition. The world needs to hear this tradition in every language, even that of the scholar.

Chapter Seven

INSTITUTIONAL AMNESIA AND THE CHALLENGE OF MOBILIZING OUR RESOURCES FOR FRANCISCAN THEOLOGY

Joseph P. Chinnici, O.F.M.

A theology worthy of its name is a spirituality that has found categories of thought adequate to its religious experience.[1]

As you know, the conference hosted by the Washington Theological Union this year, through the gracious work of Sister Ilia Delio, O.S.F., has agreed to build upon some of the developments in our scholarly family since February 11-13, 2000. At that time, scholars from different branches of the family attended a Studies Colloquium hosted by the Franciscan Institute in Aston, Pennsylvania. This was followed by a meeting between the English Speaking Conference of the Order of Friars Minor and representatives from the Franciscan study centers and other dimensions of the family (Capuchin, Conventual, Poor Clare, Third Order Regular, and Secular Franciscan Order) in Colorado Springs, in March 2000. The English Speaking Conference then established a Task Force on the Retrieval of the Franciscan Intellectual Tradition, which prepared a strategic plan for the recovery of the tradition. The plan was presented to the ministers on March 8, 2001. This Task Force Report, duly approved and adopted by the English Speaking Conference, is now available to the whole Franciscan family.

Clearly plans are taking shape that could bear great fruit for the future. These are receiving important institutional support from the various bodies. In this essay, I would like to build on this impetus by providing a few historical *caveats* and speculating a bit as to how we might mobilize our resources. My historical analysis will be primarily concerned with the pre-conciliar period. Its long shadow, whether we know it or not, continues to shape our efforts and our presuppositions.

---

[1]M.-D. Chenu, O.P., "Théologie et spiritualité," *Supplément à la "Vie Spirituelle,"* LI (1 Mai 1937): 65-70, with quotation from page 70. (Translation mine.)

Let me divide my remarks into three sections: (1) Knowing the Past so as to be Free for the Future; (2) Institutional Amnesia and Revitalization; (3) Mobilizing our Resources.

Knowing the Past so as to be Free for the Future

Have you ever wondered whether or not you were reinventing the wheel? It is a frustrating experience. In preparing for these reflections, I have had the distinct impression that we members of the Franciscan family have been running around this same circle of the retrieval of our Franciscan intellectual tradition, especially in theology, for many years. At the Franciscan Educational Conference held from August 16-19, 1954, an announcement was made from the podium: "Would all those interested in promoting a Commission for Franciscan Doctrinal Synthesis please contact Fr. Cyril Shircel, O.F.M." The membership even passed a resolution at the end of the meeting indicating that they were "aware of the need of a Franciscan doctrinal synthesis" and wanted to encourage its promoters.[2] Apparently this particular commission, with some departures and additions, some sporadic enthusiasm and intermittent despair, met over the next three years with its work culminating at the 1957 conference (August 20-22). The proceedings from that meeting contained papers emphasizing our theological tradition's contribution to reflections on the Trinity, Incarnation, the Predestination of Our Lady, "Original Justice According to St. Bonaventure," the virtues, sacramental theology, grace, the Church, and eschatology. Maurice Grajewski, O.F.M., an authority on John Duns Scotus, outlined the programmatic elements of the entire effort in his opening address, "The Concept of Franciscan Theology."

With an almost resigned sense of *déjà vu*, I read Grajewski's arguments for a "crying need for revitalization" of the Franciscan intellectual tradition in the context of the Church of his time: (1) "antiquated textbooks," "second-rate periodical articles," and "pseudo modernization of the centuries-old theological systems"; (2) the need to provide a content and method for "theology for the layman"; (3) "the equally urgent request from all sides for a theology for Sisters"; (4) the

---

[2]*Franciscan Educational Conference* XXXV (1954), 541, 545. Cyril Shircel, O.F.M., a priest of the Commissariate of the Holy Cross, received his doctorate from Catholic University with a thesis on "The Univocity of the Concept of Being in the Philosophy of John Duns Scotus" (Washington, DC: 1942).

failure to incorporate the latest scholarship, the development of dogma, and the papal teachings into seminary curricula; (5) the call of the Order of Friars Minor itself for special attention to the major themes of our Franciscan school; (6) the pressure exerted from those outside the Order for an intellectual articulation of our vision: "Seekers after truth suspect a rich treasure-trove in our vast theological literature but bewail the lack of a reliable guide through the mazes of this intricate and voluminous literary production"; (7) people's natural quest for "truth and wisdom." What Grajewski applied to sisters and seminary students could be equally said of most of the other "seekers after truth":

They are no longer satisfied with generalities, with the mouthing of the time-honored cliché of "the great Franciscan tradition," with the convenient name-dropping technique of referring to the great Franciscan masters, with the platitudes about the modernity of Franciscan doctrines which are never specifically indicated, and with the oft-repeated promise of having a Franciscan doctrinal synthesis when and if the critical edition of the *Opera Omnia* of this or that Franciscan theologian will be provided or the manuscripts of his works published or his contributions studied in the fullness of their implications. They feel, and justly so, that it can be done now.[3]

The whole conference was a stellar effort to respond to Grajewski's appeal, and, at the end of the meeting, so pleased were its participants that they established a "Commission for a Moral Synthesis."[4] The following resolutions were adopted:

3.   Whereas, this year's conference discussed sympathetically and enthusiastically a dogmatic theology according to Franciscan masters by representative members of the Franciscan family, *be it resolved* that the Franciscan Educational Conference continue to sponsor, promote, and encourage research and study leading toward an early publication of a handbook of dogmatic theology.

---

[3]Maurice Grajewski, O.F.M., "The Concept of Franciscan Theology," *Franciscan Educational Conference* XXXVIII (December 1958), 1-25, with references from pages 1-5 and long quotation from page 3.

[4]"Franciscan Approach to Theology," *Report of the Thirty-Eighth Annual Meeting of the Franciscan Educational Conference,* Our Lady Queen of Angels, Saginaw, MI, August 20-22, 1957, Franciscan Educational Conference XXXVIII (December 1958).

4. *Whereas*, in our day Franciscan and other sisterhoods, as well as the laity, realize the need for theology, *be it resolved* that the Franciscan Educational Conference sponsor and promote an adaptation of the above-mentioned dogmatic theology to meet this demand.[5]

The Thirty-eighth Conference proceedings concluded with a two page section in which the Franciscan Teaching Sisterhoods, meeting some three months later, outlined the basic tenets of the Franciscan school and called for a theology that was responsive to a sister's identity, first as a *woman*, then as a *sister*, and finally, as a *Franciscan*, so "that her apostolate may become truly Christocentric."[6]

These words are sobering for us who are gathered here almost forty-five years later to speak in the Church of our time about "The Franciscan Intellectual Tradition: Is It Meaningful Today?" They become even more sobering when you consider the fact that the participants at the 1957 conference were simply repeating a desire that had been articulated at least three times since the foundation of the Educational Conference in 1919. In 1921 the friars listened to a paper written explicitly for their gathering by Father Parthenius Minges (1861-1930), one of the leaders in the neo-Scotistic revival occurring at the time. Berard Vogt spoke on "The Origin and Development of the Franciscan School," and Edwin Auweiller tried to indicate some of the practical implications of Scotus's teachings. The proceedings commended the "splendid quarterly" *Franziskanische Studien* to "all our confreres," called for a speedy critical edition of the works of Scotus, Hales, and Bacon, and concluded with resolutions to encourage "our lectors of philosophy and theology" to enable the students "to present the ancient Scotistic doctrines in a form that will appeal to the modern mind."[7]

Throughout the 1920s there were concerted efforts to relate the major themes and orientations of Franciscan philosophy, theology, and asceticism to the educational institutions, curriculum, scientific disciplines, and pedagogical methods then developing throughout the

---

[5]"Resolutions of the Franciscan Educational Conference XXXVIII," 347.

[6]"Franciscan Teaching Sisterhoods," *Thirty-Eighth Annual Meeting of the Franciscan Educational Conference*, 349-350, with quotation from page 350.

[7]"Report of the Third Annual Meeting," *The Franciscan Educational Conference* III (December 1921), with specific references to pages 185-186.

country.[8] In 1927 Berard Vogt spoke before the third annual meeting of The American Catholic Philosophical Association on "The Franciscan School."[9] Although the 1930s saw only an occasional turn to specifically Franciscan themes, the Twenty-Fourth annual meeting of the Franciscan Educational Conference in 1942 contained a rather complete exposition of spirituality, Christology, philosophy, and psychology from the perspective of Bonaventure and Scotus.[10] We shall see the importance of this conference in part two. The seventh and eighth resolutions summarized both the advances and the difficulties of the previous two decades:

7. Whereas the just recognition of Franciscan philosophy is the earnest desire of all Franciscans, the Conference declares that the *Dictionary of Philosophy* edited by Dagobert D. Runes (Philosophical Library, N.Y., 1942), although possessing many commendable features, is uncritical in its treatment of various Franciscan topics.

8. Whereas the furtherance of genuine Franciscan doctrine requires an increased study of the original sources of Franciscan thought, be it resolved that:

1) steps be taken to make these Franciscan sources more available to scholars and students in general;

2) lectors endeavor to become better acquainted with the writings of the great exponents of Franciscan

---

[8]See for examples the proceedings of the Franciscan Educational Conference for 1922 (the teaching of history), 1924 (language study), 1926 (asceticism and spirituality), 1927 (preaching), 1929 (pedagogy, the training of teachers), 1930 (philosophy), 1931 (psychology). In particular, James O'Mahony, O.F.M.Cap., "The Franciscan School of Philosophy," *Franciscan Educational Conference* XII (November 1930), 1-14; Ephrem Longpré, O.F.M, "The Psychology of Duns Scotus and Its Modernity," *Franciscan Educational Conference* XIII (November 1931), 19-77. For excellent background on general developments in Catholic education, see Philip Gleason, *Contending with Modernity: Catholic Higher Education in the Twentieth Century* (New York: Oxford University Press, 1995).
[9]Berard Vogt, "The Franciscan School," *Proceedings of the Third Annual Meeting of the American Catholic Philosophical Association* III (1927), 113-130.
[10]See, for examples, Philibert Ramstetter, O.F.M., "Introduction to a Franciscan Spirituality," Ignatius Brady, O.F.M., "Beatitude and Psychology," Dominic Unger, O.F.M., "Franciscan Christology," all in the *Report of the Twenty-fourth Annual Meeting of the Franciscan Educational Conference*, published in *Franciscan Studies* 23 (new series, December 1942), especially the summary on pages 321-325. The address by Philotheus Boehner, O.F.M., "The Spirit of Franciscan Philosophy," was printed in *Franciscan Studies* 23 (September 1942): 217-237.

spirituality, philosophy, and theology in order to instill in their students a deeper appreciation of these Franciscan treasures;

3) a medium of exchange be established by which extant copies and editions of Franciscan works be made more accessible;

4) bibliographical information concerning noteworthy and rare Franciscan works in America be submitted for publication in *Franciscan Studies*;

5) reprints and translations especially of the most important sources of Franciscan thought be promoted.[11]

Adequate textbooks, translations, and pedagogical methods, in short, the embodiment in institutional structures of a particular approach to life, continued to be a problem in the subsequent decade. It was during this period that the class notes of Philotheus Boehner and Ignatius Brady's "blotters" (their form alone indicating the fragile nature of the undertaking and the almost sectarian features attached to Franciscan *esoterica*) began their circuitous route throughout the seminary philosophy departments of various provinces.[12] Thus, from 1921 till 1954, we find numerous summaries, profound studies, conferences, and projects—all supported by resolutions, good intentions, and some measure of success—continually repeating themselves, making with many twists and turns a kind of historical, philosophical, and theological maze in an effort to find a straight path to the Franciscan intellectual Jerusalem.

Much has happened since Minges first addressed the Franciscan Educational Conference in 1921 and since Grajewski spoke in 1954: John XXIII's *aggiornamento*; the Second Vatican Council; the social and political revolution of the 1960s; the advent of a culturally global perspective; the realignment of the clerical, religious, and lay roles in

---

[11]*Franciscan Studies*, 2 (December, 1942): 476.

[12]Philotheus Boehner, O.F.M., *The History of the Franciscan School, Part II, John of Rupella, Saint Bonaventure* (St. Bonaventure, New York, 1944, re-mimeographed at Duns Scotus College, Detroit, 1947); *Part III, Duns Scotus* (St. Bonaventure, New York, 1945, re-mimeographed at Duns Scotus College, Detroit, 1946); *Part IV, William Ockham* (St. Bonaventure, New York, 1946, re-mimeographed at Duns Scotus College, Detroit, 1946); Boehner, *Escoto el Doctor Sutil*, Pro Manuscripto (Jalisco, Mexico: Editado en Guadalajara, 1954).

the Church; the philosophical, biblical, liturgical, and theological "paradigm shifts" that truly move beyond the thought structures of a medieval mentality; the traditionalist counter-offensive; the collapse of our religious institutions of higher learning and the decline of our own communal identities; and now the pressing need for a compass in the midst of mind-boggling advances in the human sciences, technology, and geo-economic developments.

Certainly, the speakers who have gone before me, like their predecessors before them at the Educational Conferences, have attempted to address the interface between the wellsprings of our tradition and these contemporary concerns. Their case has been well stated and new avenues of approach have been articulated. But the question remains: Where do we go from here? Even more specifically, in choosing a path, can we avoid following in the footsteps of our ancestors whose own good hopes and works seem to have been ravaged by the corrosive power of change, for the most part lost in the archives of our memory, available to be trotted out only on occasions like this one? How do we, with hope in our hearts, revive and update yet again the work of generations who themselves have been ignored when it comes to the development of our own formation methods or our self-presentation as a visible and forceful public presence in the pastoral strategies of the Church? How do we draw on their valuable work for our preaching of a somewhat coherent philosophy of social and economic engagement with the world or our popularization of organs of communication that can make solid and respectable intellectual insights available to the ordinary folk whom most of us represent? In the year 2050, will someone dig up the proceedings of this meeting and ask the same question: Where did it all go? Who were these people and why did they talk like that? Franciscans do indeed make excellent buttermilk; but where is the meat, the mature food of the intellectual life?

Institutional Amnesia and
Franciscan Intellectual Revitalization

In addressing the question, where do we go from here, it seems that I should first pay attention to this sobering history of previous efforts. Why have they disappeared? *Historia magistra veritatis.* Only then can we hope to establish a useable path for the future. Clearly, there are many reasons that account for the failure of numerous well intentioned resolutions: institutional growth, the pressures of educational Americanization (standardized curriculum, accreditation procedures, professionalization), the pastoral needs of the Church, the lack of critical editions, the demand to train people in more practical fields of endeavor, the channeling of financial resources to more needy areas, the proliferation of isolated, competitive, and localized centers of learning, etc.[13] Analyzing the whole complex of events can hardly be possible without access to presently inaccessible archives. So, in what follows, let me identify what I believe are two elements affecting our past efforts at retrieval, elements that have contributed to the problem of "institutional amnesia" and the consistent and repeated loss of our tradition as a public presence among ourselves, in the Church, and in society. Unless we take these lines of development into consideration, our work for the future will appear to our contemporaries much as the eighteenth-century map that pictured Alta California as an island. To a modern cartographer, this is a period piece, sincere but ignorant, interesting but irrelevant, historic but hardly of public significance.

Retrieval within the Context
of the Church's Dominant Tradition

Previous efforts at retrieving our intellectual inheritance, initiated in the mid-nineteenth century after the devastating effects of the French Revolutionary period on the Franciscan family in Italy, Germany, France, and Spain, coincided with the overwhelming papal support for the revival of Thomism. From Leo XIII's *Aeterni Patris* of 1879 through Pius X's motu proprio *Doctoris Angelici* (June 29, 1914) and Pius XI's *Studiorum Ducem* (June 29, 1923), to Pius XII's *Humani Generis* (August 12, 1950), the doctrinal teachings of Thomas Aquinas have held pride of

---

[13]In these respects it would be good to place our own developments in the light of such works as Gleason, *Contending with Modernity*; William M. Halsey, *The Survival of American Innocence: Catholicism in an Era of Disillusionment, 1920-1940* (Notre Dame: University of Notre Dame Press, 1980); and William P. Leahy, S.J., "Catholics and Educational Expansion after 1945," in Joseph M. O'Keefe, S.J., ed., *Catholic Education at the Turn of the New Century* (New York & London: Garland Publishing, Inc., 1997), 123-154; Peter McDonough, *Men Astutely Trained, A History of the Jesuits in the American Century* (New York: The Free Press, 1992). For deeper interpretive comments, see Thomas O'Dea, *American Catholic Dilemma* (New York: Sheed & Ward, 1958); Walter J. Ong, *Frontiers in American Catholicism: Essays on Ideology and Culture* (New York: The Macmillan Company, 1961).

place in the intellectual life of the institutional Church. With the exception of the more progressive school associated with Cardinal Mercier or the historical studies of Thomas furthered by Etienne Gilson and later the Dominican school of le Saulchoir, the neo-Thomistic revival became aligned with significant forces of reaction to "modernity."[14]

In the wake of the modernist crisis, *Doctoris Angelici* in 1914 demanded adherence to the principles of St. Thomas in the metaphysical and ethical orders "on account of their value for the foundation and defense of the faith." Some individual Thomists then applied to the Sacred Congregation of Studies for approval of a list of twenty-four theses that they saw as essential to the doctrine of the great scholastic. Among the theses were Aquinas's position on the unicity of form in man, matter as the principle of individuation, and the process by which a person comes to knowledge of the singular. These are all theses in which the teaching of Thomas differs from that of Scotus.[15] Although the Sacred Congregation refused to canonize these tenets as mandatory, an essentialistic approach to truth and the theses themselves became the litmus test of orthodoxy and fidelity to the Church for many promoters of the intransigent cause. The 1917 *Code of Canon Law* explicitly affirmed the "methods, teaching, and principles" of the Angelic Doctor as those of the universal Church (c. 1366). Other schools of thought needed to be interpreted in the light of St. Thomas.

---

[14]See for very significant background Pierre Jaccard, "La Renaissance de la Pensée Franciscaine," *Revue de Théologie et de Philosophie*, XVIII (1930): 103-131; 207-233; XIX-XX (1931-1932): 168-195. On Thomas and Thomism see Pierre Thibault, *Savoir et Pouvoir, Philosophie thomiste et politique cléricale au XIXe siècle* (Québec: Les Presses de L'Université Laval, 1972); Alexander Dru, "From the *Action Française* to the Second Vatican Council, Blondel's *La Semaine Sociale de Bordeaux*," *The Downside Review*, 81 (July 1963): 226-245; Gabriel Daly, *Transcendence and Immanence* (Oxford: Clarendon Press, 1980); Emile Poulat, *Intégrisme et Catholicisme Intégral* (Paris: Casterman, 1969); Lester R. Kurtz, *The Politics of Heresy: The Modernist Crisis in Roman Catholicism* (Berkeley: University of California Press, 1986);G. Alberigo, M.-D. Chenu, E. Fouilloux, J.-P. Jossua, J. Ladrière, *Une école de théologie: le Saulchoir* (Paris: Les Editions du Cerf, 1985); Mark Schoof, *A Survey of Catholic Theology, 1800-1970* (New York: Paulist Newman Press, 1970; Joseph A. Komonchak, "Modernity and the Construction of Roman Catholicism," mss. paper in author's possession. For a fine overview of schools of neo-Thomism and their variety, see Thomas F. O'Meara, O.P., *Thomas Aquinas, Theologian* (Notre Dame: University of Notre Dame Press, 1997), 167-195. Franciscan thought was unfortunately too often formed in contrast with only the most intransigent neo-Thomism. This contrast did manage to emphasize the distinctive differences.

[15]See for background Franz Pelster, S.J., "The Authority of St. Thomas in Catholic Schools and the Sacred Sciences," *Franciscan Studies*, 13 (1953): 1-20. For comparisons with Thomas, see Berard Vogt, "The Franciscan School."

The reactionary interpreters of scholasticism among the neo-Thomists took even more strength from *Studiorum Ducem* and, despite a slight setback with the 1926 condemnation of the *Action Française*, accomplished the censure of Marie Dominique Chenu when he began to articulate his program of a "renewal of method" in the 1930s.[16] The 1950 encyclical *Humani Generis* only reinforced these more intransigent interpretations. During this whole period, of course, the seeds of a philosophical, theological, and pastoral renewal were developing that would culminate in the Second Vatican Council.[17] But the atmosphere of an official Thomism, approved by the papacy as the carrier of Catholic orthodoxy, cannot be forgotten. Firmly embedded in the institutional memory of the Church, it captured the public carriers of tradition in law, education, and speech, defined the limits of judgment, and sustained a way of interacting with the world.[18] It particularly affected the Franciscan school, its chief rival in the medieval period with a legitimate claim to orthodoxy.[19]

From the beginning of the neo-scholastic revival, the Franciscan tradition of Roger Bacon, Bonaventure, and Scotus began to be vigorously placed alongside neo-Thomism as an alternate "thought style" within the Church. The more intransigent neo-Thomists saw the two schools as completely incompatible. Scotus in particular, much more philosophically oriented and without the status of a saint, appeared the most dangerous opponent to their program. Partially in reaction to this and partially to encourage group solidarity—especially after the Leonine Union in 1897—the Franciscans tended as much as possible to differentiate Bonaventure from Thomas and to show the orthodox roots of Scotus in Bonaventure, Anselm, and Augustine. The

---

[16]Confer the important essays by Chenu, "Théologie et spiritualité," and "Dimension nouvelle de la Chrétienté," *La Vie Intellectuelle* LIII (25 Décembre, 1937): 325-351; and for interpretation, Giuseppe Alberigo, "Christianisme en tant qu'histoire et 'théologie confessante'" in *Une ecole de théologie: le Saulchoir.*

[17]See in addition to the studies mentioned above Erich Pryzwara, "Le mouvement théologique et religieux en Allemagne," *Nouvelle Revue Théologique*, 56 (1929): 565-575, 660-666; "Le Mouvement de pensee religieuse en Allemagne (1929-30)," *Nouvelle Revue Théologique*, 58 (1931): 340-348.

[18]This analysis has been greatly helped by Mary Douglas, *How Institutions Think* (Syracuse: Syracuse University Press, 1986).

[19]The Franciscan school, not a coherent whole, evolved its major positions over a long period of time, its thought being marked by the insights of individual thinkers. Confer Gian Luca Potesta, "Maestri e dottrine nel XIII secolo," Maria Pia Alberzoni, et al., eds, *Francesco d'Assisi e il primo secolo di storia francescana* (Torino: Einaudi, 1997), 307-336; and more comprehensively, Bert Roest, *A History of Franciscan Education (c. 1210-1517)* (Leiden: Brill, 2000), 185-196.

whole point about the Franciscan tradition was that it predated Aquinas and represented a wider view of reality and the Church. The friars themselves began to take the offensive in terms of an institutional presence and network of publications.[20] The critical edition of Bonaventure was accomplished between 1882-1902; the Vives edition of Scotus made its appearance at the same time, 1891-1895; *Etudes Franciscaines* began in 1893, *France Franciscaine* in 1912, *Studi Franciscani* in 1914, *Franziskanische Studien* in 1914.

Before World War I, a concerted effort argued for the beatification of Scotus, especially around the fiftieth anniversary of the promulgation of the Immaculate Conception (1854-1904).[21] The celebration of the centenary of Roger Bacon (1914) and the publication of two volumes of Alexander of Hales's *Summa* (1924-1928) continued the onslaught. In 1926, for the centenary of St. Francis, no less a person than Etienne Gilson presented a succinct but powerful exposé of the first century of Franciscan philosophy— its doctrinal synthesis rooted in the "miracle of La Verna," its debt to Augustinianism, its subordination of philosophy to a theology culminating in wisdom, its innate recognition of the limitations of reason, its refusal to see the soul simply as the "form of the body," its acceptance of a plurality of forms or *rationes seminales*, its affinity for science, and above all its focus on the goodness of God, the role of the will, and the preaching of the Gospel.[22] Parthenius Minges, Déodat de Basly, and a little later, Ephrem Longpré (1890-1965) especially embodied both the force and the limitations of the revival.[23]

For the purposes of this essay, it should be noted that Parthenius Minges became particularly important in the United States with the publication of his two articles in the *Catholic Encyclopedia* on "Duns Scotus" (V, 1909) and "Scotism and Scotists" (XIII, 1912). He addressed the Franciscan Educational Conference in 1921, and, after his death in 1930, a two-volume summary of Scotus's philosophical and

---

[20]Cf. Jaccard, "La Renaissance de la Pensée Franciscaine," part 1.

[21]See for example Mariano Fernandez Garcia, *B. Joannis Duns Scoti, Doctoris Subtilis ac Mariani, O.F.M., Vitae Compendium* (Quaracchi: Collegii S. Bonaventurae, 1907).

[22]Etienne Gilson, "La Philosophie Franciscaine," *Saint François d'Assise, Son Oeuvre-Son Influence 1226-1926* (Paris: Editions E. Droz, 1927), 148-175.

[23]See Parthenius Minges, "Joannes Duns Scotus," *Franciscan Educational Conference* III (1921), 63; Déodat de Basly, O.F.M., *Scotus Docens ou Duns Scot Enseignant la Philosophie, la Théologie, la Mystique* (Paris: La France Franciscaine, 1934); for Longpré, Edouard Parent, *Ephrem Longpré, Héraut de la Primauté du Christ et de l'Immaculée* (Montréal: Les Compagnons de Jésus et de Marie, 1985). Maurice Grajewski calls attention to these and other writers in "The Concept of Franciscan Theology," 9-10.

theological doctrines was printed—all of this without a critical edition of the medieval philosopher's writings![24] In his address to the Educational Conference meeting in West Park, Ohio, Minges noted well the polemical and defensive atmosphere in which the Franciscans were attempting to articulate their intellectual inheritance. His introductory remarks made the following points:

- There are those who say that Scotism is obsolete, which is not true. To the contrary, others speak, and rightly, of its modern value.

- It is likewise false that the Scotist School is hardly tolerated by the Church. No Scotisitc thesis has ever been condemned either by the Magisterium of the Church or by any University, including, up to now, Scotus's doctrine that the Virgin is immaculate.

- Without a doubt the Franciscan School today is belittled by many; this is much to be lamented.[25]

Minges went on to contrast Scotus and Aquinas and argue that the latter, by his wholesale adoption of Aristotle's philosophical opinions (e.g. the soul as the form of the body, matter as the principle of individuation), was much more open to erroneous interpretations. Scotus, however, even more than Aquinas, defended the individual, the knowability of things, the complete freedom of God, the dependence of the creature on the Creator. Were not Scotus's philosophical doctrines better suited to the present and future times? In addition, he argued, Scotus's theological teachings on the Trinity, the equation between charity and sanctifying grace, the sacraments and how they confer grace and forgive sins, the reality of indifferent acts, and theology as a practical science, (to name but a few of the many elements that Minges listed) were also compatible with Church teaching. In fact, did not the Franciscan view of theology with its focus on love and the will lend itself more to methods of conversion:

---

[24]Parthenius Minges, *Joannes Duns Scoti, Doctrina Philosophica et Theologica quoad res praecipuas Proposita et Exposita, I, Doctrina philosophica, Theologica fundamentalis* (Ad Claras Aquas: Collegii S. Bonaventurae, 1930); *II, Theologia specialis* (Ad Claras Aquas: Collegii S. Bonaventurae, 1930).

[25]Minges, "Joannes Duns Scotus," 50-51. (Translation mine.)

Indeed, in all Christian preaching and instruction, in every effort to convert non-Catholics, it is more necessary to stir up and encourage good will than right understanding. . . . People value life, virtue, love, religious and moral practice more than religious knowledge.

He concluded his speech with the following hardly transparent slam at the Thomistic synthesis and the reasons for its adoption by the Church:

Aquinas composed the *Summa Theologica* harmoniously and systematically, editing it in a clear order. The reasoning he presents is often less solid, and certainly less original, than the reasoning and ideas of Scotus. . . . This good, useful organization and external editorial form seem to me the chief reasons that the Church preferred Aquinas's system and recommended it with such high praise. Its external form is better, though the internal content seems quite often less laudable. Yet it is ultimately not the form, but the content that establishes truth and wins minds. Thus, I, at least, am convinced that in the future Scotus is to recover his previous fame.[26]

Yet, the specter that appeared throughout this period, despite all of the attempts to prove either the orthodoxy or the superiority of the Scotistic system, was the shadow of an institutionalized Thomism that confined the Franciscan intellectual tradition to public backwaters. The struggle can be seen in the defensive attitude and personal responses of the friars to the Church's legislation. They constantly appealed to the papacy's approval of Bonaventure, to letters from the Roman curia to Deodat de Basly, P. Chrysostome, and the Minister General, and to the support of influential curial patrons in order to stave off the Thomist attacks.[27] In 1898 Leo XIII sent a letter to the friars recalling to them their duty to follow the "common doctor." The reaction was immediate and the letter had to be clarified—there was no intention to abrogate canon 245 of the *Constitutions*, which encouraged the friars "to attach

[26]Minges, "Joannes Duns Scotus," 55-56, 62, and *passim.* (Translation mine.)
[27]See the texts in Willibrordus Lampen, O.F.M., *B. Joannes Duns Scotus et Sancta Sedes* (Ad Claras Aquas: Collegii S. Bonaventurae, 1929), 39-57.

themselves" (*inhaerere studeant*) to the teachings of the Franciscan school.[28]

At the General Chapter in 1903, the Vicar General David Fleming commended to the friars the new edition of Jerome of Montefortino's compendium of Scotus "eo quod secundum ordinem immortalis Summae Doctoris Angelici doctrina Scoti exponitur ac dilucidatur."[29] Divisive and mean-spirited struggles broke out between the two schools in the periodicals. The intransigent neo-Thomists raised constant allegations of modernism, liberalism, impiety, and heresy.[30] The 1913 *Constitutions of the Friars Minor*, while acknowledging the importance of the Franciscan philosophical and theological tradition (*ex animo inhaerere studeant*), also emphasized the great importance of Thomas ("*caeteros Scholasticos, Angelicum praesertim Doctore D. Thomas, Catholicarum Scholarum coelestem Patronum, magni faciant,*" n. 274). This was linked with the very strong article against holding any modernist opinions and was repeated in the 1914, 1921 (n. 277), 1953 (238.6) editions, and again in the 1949 *Statua pro studiis regendis in Ordine fratrum minorum* (n.60).[31]

In the 1918 *American Ecclesiastical Review*, Fulgence Meyer felt compelled to comment on the *Code of Canon Law's* prescriptions regarding Aquinas:

Evidently, however, it would be a misconstruction of its sense and drift, were one to interpret Canon 1366 so as to insist that henceforth of all the Scholastics, St. Thomas must be the only leader and the exclusive guide of Catholic professors and students in the field of philosophy and theology.

He defended the approach of Scotus with an appeal to the "variety" and "reasonable liberty which experience and history tell us they allow." In a

---

[28]Jaccard, "La Renaissance de La Pensée Franciscaine," Part 2, 221.

[29]*Acta Capituli Generalis . . . die XXX. Maji 1903* (Quaracchi: Collegii S. Bonaventurae, 1903), 56.

[30]Cf. Jaccard, "La Renaissance de La Pensée Franciscaine," Part 2, for a complete review.

[31]*Regula et Constitutiones Generales Fratrum Minorum* (Romae: Instituto Pii IX, 1913). Cf. *Regula et Constitutiones Generales Fratrum Minorum* (Quarrachi: Collegii S. Bonaventurae, 1914); *The Rule and General Constitutions of the Order of Friars Minor,* Rome: The General Curia, 1953 (Paterson, NJ: St. Anthony Guild Press, 1958); see also Franz Pelster, S.J., "The Authority of St. Thomas in Catholic Schools and the Sacred Sciences: An Opinion Regarding Two Recent Articles," with reference to page 5, footnote 13, which was actually an "Editor's note" to Pelster's article.

very telling business metaphor, Meyer wrote: "The Church is known to favor monopoly in no department of merely human activity. Monopoly means the end of honorable rivalry, soon followed by stagnation and the death of healthy enthusiasm, initiative, and energy."[32]

The struggle continued unabated. During the early 1920s, writers in *Etudes Franciscaine* carried on a running battle with Jacques Maritain regarding the orthodoxy of the Franciscan school.[33] The friars continued to appeal to the one passage in *Studiorum Ducem*, probably added by the pope himself, which seemed to allow some room for alternate systems of thinking within the Church. In 1927, when Ephrem Longpré lectured in Quebec, his presentation on Scotus was sensational, a real novelty in a stronghold where no one could obtain official approval or permission to teach or preach unless his comments were in conformity with the "last jot and tittle" of Thomas Aquinas.[34] In 1929, with the expressed approval of the Minister General and his Vicar, Willibrordus Lampen, O.F.M., published a compendium of papal comments on the orthodoxy of Scotus as a sign of legitimate "liberty of thought."

> We have the teaching of the great St. Thomas, which we have imbibed from our earliest theological studies under the guidance of our teachers, outstanding in name and dignity. But on open questions let us enjoy that freedom which the Creator of our intellect and Holy Mother Church have given us. . . . This freedom in teaching the Friars Minor have always claimed for themselves, since the Constitutions and General Chapters recommended particularly one or more of the outstanding Doctors.[35]

From the point of view of members of the American Franciscan family, much of this European wrangling and political maneuvering may have seemed inconsequential. It did however form the general context within which our own educational and formational systems developed. Neo-scholasticism, as far as the official organs of the Church went, meant neo-Thomism, and as often as not this was of the more

---

[32]Fulgence Meyer, O.F.M., "John Duns Scotus," *The Ecclesiastical Review* LVIII (June 1918): 632-650, with quotation from page 633.

[33]Jaccard, "La Renaissance de La Pensée Franciscaine," Part 2, 228-230.

[34]See Parent, *Ephrem Longpré*, 133.

[35]Lampen, *B. Joannes Duns Scotus*, 12. (Translation mine.)

intransigent party.[36]   Only more sophisticated thinkers could understand that the deeper issue at stake was not only the "plurality of forms" or the "principle of individuation," but issues of legitimate liberty of thought within the Church, the complete orthodoxy of an alternate way of approaching reality, the relationship between the faith and contemporary forces within Church and society.

In defending their inheritance, the system flowing from La Verna, the friars were intuiting something fairly profound about life. On the one hand, a philosophical tradition of Augustinianism within the atmosphere of rigid neo-Thomism meant "openness," "interiority," "dynamism," and "alternative." Etienne Gilson, in the last chapter of his famous work on Bonaventure, compared the thought of Thomas and Bonaventure and concluded with the following words:

> The philosophy of St. Thomas and the philosophy of St. Bonaventure are complementary, as the two most comprehensive interpretations of the universe as seen by Christians, and it is because they are complementary that they never either conflict or coincide.[37]

On the other hand, philosophy—the articulation of fundamental presuppositions about reality, the role of critical thought in human progress, the ability to assimilate new developments, how one knows the world, how the infinite and finite intersect, how universals and particulars are related—was the terrain on which the battles over modernity would continue to be fought, even if at times the battle itself often degenerated into in-house squabbling. Maurice Blondel, influenced as he was by Augustine, recognized what was at stake very early in his career. "And since the thomist [the manualist] starts from principles which, for the most part, are disputed in our time," he wrote:

> Since he does not offer the means of restoring them by his method; since he presupposes a host of assertions which are just

---

[36]See the fine set of essays in Philip Gleason, *Keeping the Faith: American Catholicism Past and Present* (Notre Dame, IN: University of Notre Dame Press, 1987), especially pp. 11-34, 136-151.

[37]Etienne Gilson, *The Philosophy of St. Bonaventure*, trans. Dom Illtyd Trethowan and Frank J. Sheed (Paterson, NJ: St. Anthony Guild Press, 1965), 449. For the importance of Augustine's thought, see in particular Erich Przywara, S.J., "St. Augustine and the Modern World," trans. E. I. Watkin, ed. M. C. D'Arcy, S.J., et al., *A Monument to Saint Augustine* (London: Sheed & Ward, 1945), 251-286.

those which are nowadays called in question; since he cannot provide, in his system, for the new requirements of minds which must be approached on their own ground, one must not tend to treat this triumphant exposition as the last word. We are still in the life of struggle and suffering; and to understand this is itself a good and a gain. We must not exhaust ourselves refurbishing old arguments and presenting an *object* for acceptance while the *subject* is not disposed to listen. It is not divine truth which is at fault but human preparation, and it is here that our effort should be concentrated. And it is not just an affair of adaptation or temporary expediency; for this function of subjective preparation is of the first importance; it is essential and permanent, if it is true that man's action co-operates all along the line with that of God.[38]

It was precisely to address this problem that the Dominican school of Le Saulchoir, so aware of the dynamic and historic element in the thought of Thomas, had arisen in the mid-1930s. The fundamental themes of M.-D. Chenu's work critiqued a scholasticism that was a-historical and polemic, expressed the urgency of facing the problem of the historicity of the faith, and urged the reuniting of theology and spirituality. In 1938 Chenu was forced to adhere to a set of propositions the Roman authorities placed before him, and in 1940 a public attack came in the form of a long article against those who "pretended to promote theological renewal" and subjectivism. Particularly problematic were the development of an ecclesiology which saw the Church as a prolongation of the Incarnation, the promotion of ecumenism, and the open discussion of the purposes of marriage. Condemnation came in 1942.[39]

Whether or not friars were aware of these difficulties, certainly the battles with which they were engaged can hardly be interpreted outside this same historical trajectory. In June 1942, the friars attending the twenty-fourth annual Franciscan Educational Conference heard talks

---

[38]Maurice Blondel, *The Letter on Apologetics and History and Dogma*, texts prepared by Alexander Dru and Illtyd Trethowan, (New York: Holt, Rinehart and Winston, 1964), 146-147. Blondel would also independently incline towards the absolute primacy of Christ, a position with historic roots in Duns Scotus. See Jacques Flamand, *L'Idée de Médiation chez Maurice Blondel* (Louvain: Editions Nauwelaerts, 1969), 203-211; Henri Bouillard, *Blondel and Christianity* (Washington: Corpus Books, 1969), 201-202,
[39]Alberigo, "Christianisme en tant qu'Histoire et 'Theologie Confessante,'" *Une école de théologie: le Saulchoir*, 12-15, 22-23.

grouped under the general heading: "Basic Trends of the Franciscan School." Philotheus Boehner gave one of the most stimulating speeches entitled "The Spirit of Franciscan Philosophy."[40] Critiques of a moribund scholasticism, a turn to history, openness to modernity, and a search for unity between theology and life permeated the address. This intellectual leader in the United States first chastised friars who sought simply to reduce Franciscanism to its Augustinian elements. There could just as well be an "Aristotelian Franciscanism." Diversity, complexity, "wealth of personalities and doctrines"—not simply a set of preconceived theses—marked the school. Boehner sought to move to the heart of the intellectual endeavor, to find its unity by identifying four characteristics permeating the "entire Franciscan tradition." Here only a summary need be given:

> (1) *Franciscan philosophy is critical.* Marked by a "sound Christian distrust in a purely natural philosophical enterprise," the epistemological corollary of the distinction between the *potentia Dei ordinata* and the *potentia Dei absoluta*, especially in Scotus, "has the happy faculty of eliminating all those faulty demonstrations that ignore contingency in this world." Such critical thinking also leads to a refusal to confuse or mix the disciplines of theology and philosophy: "A revealed truth transported from theology into supposedly philosopohic demonstration, and masquerading all the while as a philosophic fact—that is a theologism. Theological in reality and philosophical in appearance, it is a hybrid; and with such hybrids, our modern manuals and textbooks are fairly bulging." Boehner gave two examples of "theologisms," both from Aquinas—identifying the *primum ens* with God too quickly and pretending to prove the immortality of the soul philosophically.
>
> (2) *Franciscan philosophy is scientific.* Here Boehner described two general types of philosophy—"philosophy as wisdom," of which Augustine and Bonaventure were examples, and "philosophy as science," represented by Scotus and Ockham. Boehner clearly defined the latter as true Franciscan philosophy; what was

---

[40]Philotheus Boehner, O.F.M., "The Spirit of Franciscan Philosophy," *Franciscan Studies*, 33 (September 1942): 217-237. The summary quotations below may be found within the respective subdivisions of the article.

needed today was a return to the rigor of Aristotelian thinking:
"Is it not just this lack of Aristotelian method that has brought
Neo-Scholasticism into disrepute? While respectful lip-service
is paid to the truth of the statement that a true conclusion does
not imply the truth of the reasoning, how often it is ignored in
practice."

(3) *Franciscan philosophy is progressive*, always identified by a "close
contact with the general standard of scientific thinking." At this
point, Boehner launched a general attack on neo-scholasticism:
"That [progressive] spirit has been killed in the Neo-Thomistic
School which, more than any other school, has fostered an
opposite spirit of blind, stubborn exclusiveness. But Neo-
Scotists are certainly in no position to throw stones. They too
have been false to a better spirit." In contract, Franciscan
thinkers "believed in progress"; "they enjoyed and exercised
their right of freedom, namely to submit to convincing reasons,
not to the weight of any authority unless it was directly or
indirectly divine"; "They were free of that intellectual pride
responsible for exclusive, idolatrous attachment to the doctrine
of a single school, and they saw that the achievement of truth
comes from the combined effort of all those who love truth."
The history of philosophy manifested two "equally obnoxius
extremes": "that fossilizing process peculiar to the narrow
'School' spirit"; the abandonment of "our tradition altogether."
In a remarkable comment on the general attitude in the
textbooks of his time, Boehner concluded: "Too often we
combat modern enemies with weapons that have only one
claim to value, their age. They are old, indeed, but they are not
efficient. We are, at present, face to face, with Materialism and
Atheism, Positivism and Behaviorism, Pragmatisim and
Evolutionism. Taken as a whole, they constitute a formidable
threat against the foundations of true Scholasticism.
Nevertheless, they do contain many elements that could be of
great use to Progressive Scholasticism, and they do take
complete advantage of the higher scientific standard of our
times."

(4) *Franciscan philosophy is practical.* Appealing to Bonaventure's
treatise on the *Seven Gifts of the Spirit*, Boehner argued that the

ultimate purpose of science was edification; knowledge and love needed to be combined. In the act of contemplation, "the will in the act of love, represents a higher value than the intellect." An edifying science, one that admitted the limits of human reason, produced the fruits of humility (over against animosity and contempt of others) and charity. "Our philosophical studies and teaching," he challenged his listeners, "will be determined essentially by our apostolic task. We are not pure philosophers, neither do we train our students to become pure philosophers. It is not for our own benefit alone that we study; our philosophical activity too, is inspired by the example of St. Francis: 'non sibi soli vivere sed aliis proficere. . . .'"

In approaching the topic in this fashion, Philotheus Boehner clearly de-centered the ahistorical concentration that had developed in the Franciscan intellectual revival as it defined itself over against the dominant neo-Thomism. If the battleground of modernity was philosophy and the Church's relationship with the world, this preeminent teacher argued for an interface between the true inner spirit of Franciscanism and contemporary currents of thought, contemporary problems in the world. Fond of quoting Scotus but without denying Bonaventure's contribution, he broke the ground which Allan Wolter has so successfully negotiated up to our own time: *"In processu generationis humanae semper crevit notitia veritatis."*[41] Here was a genuine tradition of openness that the participants in the 1942 conference hoped to make available to "the needs and life of the common people."[42]

As we have seen, this program of revitalization, as fecund as it could have been, remained to a large extent peripheral in the language, self-identity, pastoral action, and public institutional structures of both the Church and the Order in the United States. There were clearly some attempts to filter the insights of the Franciscan school into the activities and mentality of the friars, but the comments made by the anonymous author of a 1948-1949 booklet on "The Sacraments According to the

---

[41]See Boehner, "The Spirit of Franciscan Philosophy," 230 referring to Ord. IV., d.1, q.3, n.8. For Wolter's use of the same insight see Allan B. Wolter, O.F.M., *The Philosophical Theology of John Duns Scotus*, ed. Marilyn McCord Adams (Ithaca, NY: Cornell University Press, 1990), 162.

[42]Remarks of Thomas Plassmann, O.F.M., in "Basic Trends of the Franciscan School," *Franciscan Educational Conference*, 1942, *Franciscan Studies*, 2 (December 1942): 324; confer also the resolutions on page 476.

Franciscan School" captured both the desires of many teachers and the overwhelming odds against accomplishing the goal of change:

> There has been noted in recent years a very definite danger of stressing external observance in Catholic life, concomitant lack of emphasis on the true interior adaptation. Thus our American Catholics have been termed sacramental Catholics in a derogatory sense. We believe that the Franciscan theologians have a great deal to offer towards a well balanced appreciation of these great gifts of God, the sacraments. . . .
>
> Finally, a word of warning to the reader. The following pages have not been written in any partisan spirit as if to derogate from the just claims of any other school in the Catholic Church. We simply believe that the philosophers and theologians who followed in the footsteps of the Seraph of Assisi have much to offer Catholic philosophy and theology, and consequently their contributions should find a place in any well-rounded ascetico-mystical treatises.[43]

The 1950 encylical of Pius XII, *Humani Generis*, would once again force a defensive posture on the part of those arguing for a diversity of intellectual schools within the tradition.[44]

In 1958, *The Cord* carried a translation of a significant article written five years previously by Marianus Mueller, O.F.M.[45] In a two-part discussion designed to identify both what was wrong with the intellectual enterprise of his day and also how theology could be renewed, this German Franciscan pretty well summarized the growing dissatisfaction of many with "the usual, customary Christianity with its external, unfruitful activity." He looked to Franciscan sources to establish equilibrium in the Church. What was needed, once again, was a return to the thought of Scotus: "The goal proper to theology is not the dispelling of ignorance. Theology should ever again unravel and

---

[43]"The Sacraments According to the Franciscan School," Pro Manuscripto, The Franciscan Fathers, 1500 34th Avenue, Oakland 1, CA, n.d., p. 1.

[44]See Franz Pelster, S.J., "The Authority of St. Thomas in Catholic Schools and the Sacred Sciences."

[45]Benedict Leutenegger, O.F.M., "What's Wrong with Our Theology?" *The Cord*, 8 (April 1958): 104-114; "The Renewal of Our Theology," *The Cord*, 8 (May 1958): 136-146. The articles are a translation of the original by Marianus Mueller. Quotations are taken from pages 137 (referring to Scotus, Ord., prol., p 5, q. 2, n. 355 [Rome 1950]), and the respective sections analyzing the deficiencies. The quotation on "customary Christianity" (page 105) is taken from Bishop Landersdorfer, and the one on Luther (page 109) comes from a 1950 article by Sophronius Clasen.

explain the truths of Faith so that the hearer can more effectively put into practice what is presented to him." Mueller identified four major deficiencies in contemporary theology:

- *Religious intellectualism*, in which the truths of the faith are presented but "the personal and subjective, the life lived by Faith and by trust in God through Jesus Christ, is omitted."
- *Deistic activism*, in which people by their own actions seek "through the knowledge of the faith to force some decision in matters of belief." "This extreme activism brings about the type of ethical man, in contrast to the religious man who grows in true submission to God."
- *Separation of theology from life*, in which "the all too rationalistic and positivistic theology of today with its express purpose of merely understanding the truth is directed to the real and objective and not to that which is personal and character forming.
- *Impoverishment from a one-sided theology*: "Our theology for a long time has been determined too strongly by its counter-attack against Luther. Thereby it becomes one-sided in many of its teachings. The truths which Luther overstressed were permitted to recede too far back, although they were fundamental tenets of the Gospel, e.g. unmerited grace, the insufficiency of human effort without Christ's redeeming grace, "the redeeming strength of the word of God, the universal priesthood of the faithful, the true liberty of a Christian within every kind of law and holiness by good works. . . . Is it not time that our theology and our practical Christian way of life step out of its anti-Lutheran, protesting attitude—and that for the sake of our own selves?"

Mueller's call was nothing less than for a mainstreaming of the major tenets of the Franciscan intellectual tradition, a return to "Seraphic theology," but as with the many commentators who preceded him, his program needed an institutional base which was not his to give. Its obvious affinity with some of the tenets of Luther's reform hardly spoke for its general acceptance! Still, it was a beginning.

In terms of an opening towards an institutional presence in the intellectual life and pastoral activity of the Church and the Order, the real opportunity for the tradition came with the Second Vatican Council. It was too late. From April 21-23, 1966, a symposium was held to commemorate the seventh centenary of the birth of John Duns Scotus. Sisters and friars, religious and lay, gathered at Duns Scotus College to hear numerous scholars discourse on "Scotus Speaks Today." Most notably, Charles Balic, O.F.M., addressed the participants on "Duns Scotus in the Present Moment of the Church." Just three months later, Paul VI issued his Apostolic Letter *Alma Parens* (July 14, 1966), on, among other things, the relevance of Scotus for the ecumenical endeavor.[46] The huge international congresses held on Scotus (1966) and Bonaventure (1974) within a few years of each other furthered the interface between the tradition and the contemporary world.[47] However, the real force of renewal went in another direction.

Moving in counter reaction to the formalistic thought of the previous decades, people turned towards Biblical and liturgical sources within the Church and formed a public discourse shaped by the human sciences and ever increasing social and global needs. The insular world of the Latin Middle Ages, the so-called world of abstract metaphysical speculation reflected in the academic infighting and mimeographed notes of the 1930s to 1950s, had ceased to speak to people. The mental furniture and Christian culture that it presupposed had disappeared at

---

[46]See *Scotus Speaks Today, 1266-1966, Seventh Centenary Symposium* (Southfield, Michigan: Duns Scotus College, 1968) and Charles Balic, O.F.M., "Duns Scotus in the Present Moment of the Church," in the same volume, pp. 11-63, where he relates the great liberty the Council encouraged. He also narrates the emotional reaction of Etienne Gilson ("This is a great day! This was known, but it needed to be said!") when Paul VI said that the Church did not wish to impose Aquinas as the exclusive authority nor limit the legitimate diversity of intellectual schools and systems of thought (p. 27). Balic analyzes the history of the move away from Aquinas as the sole teacher in the first few pages of his article. For *Alma Parens* see *Franciscan Studies*, 27 (1967): 5-10, and particularly the remarks of the Apostolic Delegate to Great Britain, H. E. Cardinale, on "The Significance of the Apostolic Letter . . . ," pp. 11-20.

[47]For examples, *De Doctrina Joannis Duns Scoti, Acta Congressus Scotistici Internationalia Oxonii et Edimburgi, 11-17 Sept., 1966 celebrati*, Vols. I-IV (Romae: 1968); John K. Ryan, Bernardine M. Bonanesa, eds., *John Duns Scotus, 1265-1965, Studies in Philosophy and the History of Philosophy*, Volume 3 (Washington DC: The Catholic University of America Press, 1965); A. Pompei, ed., *San Bonaventura Maestro di Vita Francescana e di Sapienza Cristiana, Atti del Congresso Internazionale per il VII Centario di San Bonaventura da Bagnoregio* (Roma: Pontificia Facolta Teologica "San Bonaventura," 1976), I-III; Jacques Guy Bougerol, et al., *S. Bonaventura 1274-1974* (Roma: Collegio S. Bonaventura, I, 1972; II-III, 1973; IV-V, 1974); Pascal F. Foley, ed., *Proceedings of the Seventh Centenary Celebration of the Death of Saint Bonaventure* (New York: The Franciscan Institute, 1975).

least fifteen years before the end of the Council. It was an irony of history that a real institutional opening occurred precisely when the intellectual landscape and the structures of formation and education were changing in such a way in the United States as to divert both attention and resources in other directions. The infra-structure that could possibly have supported an institutional presence disappeared, seemingly overnight. Bonaventure and Olivi, Scotus, Lull, and Ockham were fine, but "no one lived there anymore." What was it they were trying to say, anyway? But before we get to that point in our story—which is where we come in—we need first very briefly to indicate one other characteristic of our inheritance supporting the "institutional amnesia" which derailed our predecessors.

Retrieval within the Context of Containment

Over and over again in the expositions of the Franciscan intellectual tradition, our predecessors identified what they called its "practical" orientation. What Minges said in 1921, Boehner affirmed in 1942; what Mueller spoke in 1953, Grajewski emphasized in 1957:

Hence, Franciscan theology results in a body of living and dynamic doctrine. For the major part, theology for the friars is not the speculative theorizing about abstracted essences and hypothetical solutions, but a constant striving to mould into practical teaching the revealed realities of the deposit of Catholic faith. Practicality and actuality, not theory and possibility constitute its focal point. It simply strives to mirror the life of the faithful in the life of our Lord as recorded in the Gospels and tradition.[48]

The commentators discovered the historical and philosophical foundations for this approach in the biblical foundations of Franciscan thought, the life of Francis himself, the influence of Augustinianism, the focus on the primacy of the will and charity, the centrality of Christ, and the pursuit of wisdom. Certainly, theology culminating in wisdom

---

[48]Grajewski, "The Concept of Franciscan Theology," 24; see Minges, "Joannes Duns Scotus," 55: "Sed per se theologia tota petit fines practicos, vitam Deo placentem et cum Deo unitam tum in terra tum in coelo. Immo fides ipsa minus dependet a cognitione recta quam a voluntate bona et vita morali, secut scriptura frequenter et indubie docet." For Boehner, confer above.

was an earmark of Bonaventure's thought; but so also, Scotus argued even in the intellectual order for the primacy of charity. Against Aristotle, Scotus made his own the view of his predecessors: "Se contra hoc arguit alius philosophus noster, scilicet Paulus, qui dicit quod charitas excellentior est."[49] This being the case, one would expect there to be close connections between an intellectual reflection that issued in personal participation in love, formational structures, and pastoral challenges. Philosophy, theology, spirituality, and mission would thus be united in the Franciscan universe. Was this not the vision of Bonaventure himself?

Yet, all of the scholars and educators whom we have mentioned seemed to have labored not only under the burden of a dominant tradition that suspected their orthodoxy but also within the confines of a lifestyle that contained the explosive communal and pastoral potential of their own tradition. The "spirit of Franciscan philosophy"—critical, scientific, progressive, practical—definitely existed, but it could have no real institutional incarnation. For what exactly would happen to the entire system, to religious obedience, to educational pedagogy, to preaching, to the care of souls, to the relationship with the world, to ecclesiology and moral theology, if some of the Franciscan principles were applied?

One example of this particular problem of containment can be given. At the Franciscan Educational Conference in 1921, Edwin Auweiler, O.F.M., gave a long discourse on "The Bearing of Scotistic Doctrines on Practical Theology."[50] "Where in our colleges and Seminaries," he asked, "is the Professor that will urge upon his students the riding of some Scotistic hobby or the deeper investigation of some peculiarly Scotistic tenet?" Students seemed merely to recite textbook answers and eventually deliver "platitudinous" sermons.

Had students been trained in the stern school of Scotus' inexorable Logic, we would not have to deplore the absurd views on the relation between Church and State; the

---

[49]As quoted in Boehner, *Escoto, El Doctor Sutil*, 173, with reference to Rep. IV., d. 49, q. 2, n. 23; t. 24, p. 625. For a contemporary interpretation of the importance of this, see Mary Beth Ingham, "Duns Scotus, Morality and Happiness: A Reply to Thomas Williams," *American Catholic Philosophical Quarterly*, LXXIV (Spring 2000): 173-195.

[50]Edwin Auweiler, O.F.M., "The Bearing of Scotistic Doctrines on Practical Theology." *Franciscan Educational Conference* III (December 1921), 150-179, with long quotation from page 151.

incompetence of so many to speak with authority on the great questions of the day; the un-Christian and un-Evangelical emphasis on racial and national conceits and prejudices; the trivial and exploded theories on re-construction and social betterment propagated from many a Catholic pulpit.

Auweiler went on to argue for adopting the Louvain school of neo-Scholasticism with its emphasis on the use of the vernacular, avoidance of the syllogistic form of argumentation ("which serves as a formal training in dialectics rather than for the expansion of mental culture"), recognition of "full rights to the experimental sciences," and the development of an historical sense. Here was a pedagogical scheme with far-reaching implications. It was never realized in any integrated fashion.

Auweiler also noted a number of Scotus's teachings in moral theology that seemed to be particularly important: the possibility of an indifferent act, the unity between intention and action in the human being, the role of conscience, the vindication of human liberty in following probable opinions. But after searching far and wide in the textbooks to see how Scotistic principles had been applied in liturgy, pastoral theology, canon law, moral theology, and the interpretation of spirituality, he could find little influence beyond a few fine points of scholastic argumentation. Still, it seemed to him that the Primacy of Christ and the Sovereign Freedom of the Will had particular application in times which rejected the divinity of Christ, times marked by "unprecedented social unrest and discontent." How could one move this beautiful word of the tradition from the heart of the specialists through the pastoral textbooks to the people in the pews?[51]

---

[51]In the comments that followed Auewiler's speech (181-184), some of the participants pointed out other areas where they thought Scotus's teaching could be practically applied: the focus on intentionality and will as an important factor in "determining the moral goodness of an act"; an emphasis on the love of God for us; our own happiness as rooted in our love for God. This orientation, Fr. Philip argued, would "take away much of that dryness and sameness from the first part of the retreat of which so many religious complain." In considering sin, it would also be best to interpret it as an "aversion from God and a conversion to creatures," a repudiation of our "highest good." "By abandoning our highest good we relinquish "lasting happiness" and thus the sinner becomes his own executioner. This thought has as much power to draw us from sin as the thought that sin is rebellion against God, which rebellion the Justice of God is constrained to punish." In the *via illuminativa* "the love of the God Man should be the burden of all our discourses—his "amor affectivus" in the hidden life, his "amor effectivus" in his public life."

Throughout the thirty years that would follow Auweiler's speech, the friars searched for numerous ways to integrate their philosophy and theology with their quest for perfection and pastoral activities, especially in the fields of sacramental theology, the virtues, and growth in the Christian life.[52] But retrospectively, they seem to have been merely dusting off a few parts of an antiquated system. It is abundantly obvious that the annual Franciscan Educational Conferences dealing with preaching (1927), pedagogy (1929), seminaries (1932), social life (1933), religious instruction (1937), the youth movement (1938), liturgy (1939), moral guidance (1949), law and government (1950), problems in education (1952), and theology in daily life (1953) referred only tangentially to the application of basic Franciscan principles to real life situations. Papal pronouncements, Catholic Action motifs, obedience to the law, adaptation to the secular standards of education, the needs of institution building, a sacrificial asceticism focused on the purgative way seem to have controlled the discussion. Containment, both self-imposed and presupposed, was the order of the day. Principles could be articulated but their implications and implementation within a larger "system of the sacred" remained either elusive or spiritualized.[53]

Within the context of the Church of the early twentieth century, Bonaventure was forced to migrate into that section on the shelf called "ascetical and mystical theology." Scotus became the preeminent "Doctor marialis," and key doctrines such as the primacy of Christ and the centrality of charity came to be communicated in the language of popular spirituality and devotion. [54] Scotus's "good pagan," who could

---

[52]See for good examples Philibert Ramstetter, O.F.M., "Introduction to a Franciscan Spirituality," *Franciscan Studies*, 23 (December 1942): 326-367, 24th Annual Franciscan Educational Conference; Franciscan Clerics, *The Virtues According to the Franciscan School* (Old Mission Santa Barbara, Summer 1946); Aidan Mullaney, T.O.R., "The Infused Virtues According to the Franciscan School," and Ernest Latko, O.F.M., "A Cursory Survey of the Franciscan Contribution to Sacramental Theology," in *Franciscan Approach to Theology, Franciscan Educational Conference* XXXVIII (December 1958), 176-245.

[53]A general analysis of this context would take this essay too far afield, but it must be asked what was the interior relationship between the principles of the Franciscan intellectual tradition and dominant themes within the American Catholic Church, for example, the juridicism occasioned by the Church-State polemics or the "triumph of the purgative way." Confer for background, Joseph P. Chinnici, O.F.M., *Living Stones, The History and Structure of Catholic Spiritual Life in the United States* (Maryknoll, NY: Orbis Books, second edition, 1996); Robert A. Orsi, "'Mildred, is it fun to be a cripple?' The Culture of Suffering in Mid-Twentieth Century American Catholicism," in Thomas J. Ferraro, ed., *Catholic Lives/Contemporary America, The South Atlantic Quarterly*, 93 (Summer 1994): 547-590.

[54]Pierre Jaccard, "La Renaissance de la Pensée Franciscaine," article III. As examples see Leonardus M. Bello, "Litterae encyclicae de Universali Christi Primatu atque

be the object of God's gracious liberality, disappeared from the radar screen.[55] How many preachers spoke lovingly of the "crib, the cross, and the eucharist," without conveying in the least that these central symbols of Franciscan thought were in fact a "dangerous memory" capable of reimagining the social and ecclesial orders?[56]

From the point of view of the contemporary historian, this reality of a containment that set the boundaries for the implementation of thought seems to have been primarily shaped by two very particular realities: the understanding of religious life and the attitude towards the social, political, and economic conditions of the world. Let me say a brief word about each of them. The nineteenth century revival of Franciscan religious life took place under a restorationist philosophy and relied for its sources on the juridical and moral commentaries of the eighteenth century. In Spain, the practice of the evangelical counsels, linked with a perfectionistic view of religious life, took center stage. As one author puts it,

> Strictness in practice keeps a tight connection with the strict-
> ness present in morality. The disputes of the seventeenth
> century between the probabalists and the probabiliorists find
> their followers and partisans in the eighteenth century among
> the expositors of the teaching regarding the regular life. These
> expositors apply to the practices of religious life the principles
> of moral tutiorism to explain the perfectionist approach that
> they hold. They establish probabiliorism as the sole practical
> rule of conduct for those who aspire to perfection.[57]

The restoration in Italy was also such that a return to the ordinary disciplines (silence, celebration of the liturgy, mental prayer, reading

---

Regalitate," *Acta Ordinis Fratrum Minorum*, LII (1933): 293-311; R. P. Déodat de Basly, O.F.M., *Le Sacré-Coeur, Selon Le Bienheureux Jean Duns Scot* (Paris: Editions Franciscaines, 5th edition, 1946).

[55]"Prologue of the Ordination of John Duns Scotus," 54-56, in Allan B. Wolter, O.F.M., trans., "Duns Scotus on the Necessity of Revealed Knowledge," *Franciscan Studies*, XI (Sept.-Dec. 1951): 231-272.

[56]The concept of "dangerous memory" is taken from expositions in Johann Metz, *A Passion for God*, trans. J. Matthew Ashley (New York: Paulist Press, 1998); James Matthew Ashley, *Interruptions, Mysticism, Politics and Theology in the Work of Johann Baptist Metz* (Notre Dame, IN: University of Notre Dame Press, 1998).

[57]Translation mine. For a full exposition, see Gaspar Calvo Moralejo, O.F.M., "Teologia de la Vida Religiosa en La Restauración de la Orden Franciscana en España (1863-1856), *Archivo Ibero-Americano*, 44.173-174 (Enero-Junio 1984): 5-101, with quotation from page 96.

during meals, horarium, enclosure) and a return to community life became the central project both of the Church and leaders within the Order. An individual such as Bernardino da Portogruaro was well versed in the thought of Bonaventure and emphasized both a Trinitarian theology and the participation by the individual in the life of the Spirit. Devotion to the Sacred Heart became a large element in his agenda, as did a critical edition of the sources and the establishment of a solid educational system.[58] But given the general principles of the Leonine Union, the importance of one central legislation and the convergence of these mentalities with the battles surrounding modernism, the key virtues governing religious life focused more and more on obedience to authority, enclosure, and the keeping of the Rule.[59] A good example of the overall perfectionist and moralistic approach, with its roots in the reaction against modernism, can be found in an article in the 1913 Constitutions which was repeated continually through the 1953 edition:

Lectoribus et Fratribus quibuscumque in virtute sanctae obedientiae prohibetur ne publice vel privatim docere, defendered vel approbare audeant doctrinam vel sententiam aliquam erroream, suspectam, vel quomodocumque Modernismum spaientem, aut bonis moribus contrariam; immo caveant a nimia opinonum licentia, praecipue in doctrinis ad mores pertinentibus. Quapropter magis comunes, magisque probatas catholicorum sententias sequi, atque sanctae Sedis Decretis ex corde se conformare omnio tenentur.[60]

After the 1917 Code of Canon Law was enacted, religious life became homogenized, a trend that encouraged this general orientation.

---

[58]See in particular Giuseppe Buffon, O.F.M., "Prospettive e Problema della Storia dell'ordine dei Frati Minori nel Secondo Ottocento," *Archivum Franciscanum Historicum*, 90 (1997): 535-585; Buffon, *Il Tempo di Bernardino da Portogruaro* (Assisi: Edizioni Porziuncula, 1997).

[59]Confer Maurice Carmody, "I Quattro Principi dell'Unione Leonina 1897: Sfondo e Contesto," *Antonianum*, LXXIII (Januarius-Martius 1998): 79-109; Romain Georges Mailleux, "La Legislazione dell'Ordine dei Frati Minori Dopo L'Unione Leonina: Sussulti, Progressi, Questioni," *Antonianum*, LXXIII (Januarius-Martius 1998): 111-130.

[60]*Regula et Constitutiones* (1913), # 275; see *The Rule and General Constitutions of the Order of Friars Minor* (Rome: General Curia, 1953), #239: "The Lectors are forbidden in virtue of holy obedience to dare to teach, defend or approve publicly or privately any erroneous or suspect doctrine or opinion, or one which in any way savors of Modernism, or is opposed to good morals; indeed they shall beware of too great liberty of opinion, especially in doctrines pertaining to morals. For this reason they are absolutely obliged to follow the more common and more approved opinion of Catholics and to conform sincerely to the instructions of the Holy See."

Within the Order of Friars Minor, the friars became more allied with parochial ministry. The demands of this service created tensions with their lifestyle, which in turn reinforced the insistence of authority that the friars "keep the Rule" and conform to the common law of the Church. Adaptation occurred, but only in a piecemeal fashion.[61] Certainly, the commentaries on the Rule used in the United States, typical of the interpretations also offered for the Third Order Regular Rule, followed a similar focus on regularity, obedience, and sticking to the safe path both internally and externally.[62] It is no wonder that when Cajetan Esser wrote his reflections on the Rule in 1965 he identified "three basic factors" that had obscured its true interpretation: "the influence of legend, which in any given situation often proves an obstacle to the attainment of historical truth; the influence of asceticism, which is quick to give a "pious" interpretation to everything; and the influence of law, often in the form of a frightening legalism, which had especially baneful repercussions in the area under consideration."[63] Only in the light of this overwhelming tendency towards the formal construction of reality can the significance of Pacificus Peratoni's 1950 renewal encyclical on Franciscan spirituality be fully appreciated.[64] It seemed a liberation, but it also reflected a world in which spirituality, removed from real life, took on surprisingly general characteristics.

---

[61]For background see Benedikt Mertens, "Franciscans and Parochial Ministry: Past and Present Aspects of a Debated Question," *Antonianum*, LXXV (Julius-September 2000): 523-554. As examples see the legislation for the Santa Barbara province: *Ordinationes Provinciales, Provinciae Sanctae Barbarae* (Fruitvale, CA, 1922); *Ordinationes Provinciales Provinciae Californiensis S. Barbarae Ordinis Fratrum Minorum* (San Francisco, 1941). One of the best overall interpretations which sets the American context for these developments is Jay P. Dolan, R. Scott Appleby, Patricia Byrne, and Debra Campbell, *Transforming Parish Ministry: The Changing Roles of Catholic Clergy, Laity, and Women Religious* (New York: Crossroad, 1989).
   [62]Confer for examples, A Priest of the English Province, *The Rule of St. Francis . . . The Religious Vows and the Rule* (London: Salesian Press, revised edition, 1935); Rev. John Ilg, O.F.M., *Explanation of the Rule of the Friars Minor* (n.p, 1927). Ilg wrote from the Franciscan novitiate, Teutopolis, IL.
   [63]Esser, *Rule and Testament of St. Francis, Conferences to the Modern Followers of Francis* (Chicago: Franciscan Herald Press, 1977), 7. As one example of Third Order Regular developments tending to follow a very generalized pattern, see Gian Ackermans, Ursula Ostermann, O.S.F., Mary Serbacki, O.S.F., eds., *Called by God's Goodness, A History of the Sisters of St. Francis of Penance and Christian Charity in the Twentieth Century* (Stella Niagara, NY: The Sisters of Saint Francis of Penance and Christian Charity, 1997)
   [64]Most Rev. Fr. General Pacific M. Perantoni, O.F.M., *Franciscan Spirituality, The Encyclical Letteer Centenaria Solemnia*, May 21-June 4, 1950 (Chicago: Franciscan Herald Press, 1950). See also Valentin Breton, O.F.M., *Franciscan Spirituality* (NY; Desclee Company, 1960), which follows along the same lines.

This containment of the intuition and the intellectual charism within the inherited structures of religious life contributed in several ways to the "institutional amnesia" that I have tried to identify. First of all, Franciscans themselves, as often as not, related ambiguously on the intellectual level to the ideals and aspirations of the *poverello*. The publicly dubious nature of Scotus's orthodoxy combined with the interpretive legacy of Paul Sabatier and the words of the saint himself to encourage the friars to authenticate their approach to reality by idealizing their founder. Francis became both a *vir Catholicus* and a true *simplex et idiota*. With Bonaventure confined to spirituality, Scotus exiled, and Ockham identified as the forerunner of the Reformation, Francis the unlearned became the sole formational norm. Any sense that the theological and philosophical reflections of his successors stood in continuity with his intuition and experience lost credibility. Did he not have an ambiguous attitude towards studies? What did the Rule say about learning? Was he not always obedient to ecclesiastical authority? How could the institutional demands of education fit with the practice of seraphic poverty? Had not Bonaventure clericalized and monasticized the Order, thus abandoning the primitive ideal? Questions such as these, nagging at the periphery of the self-image and identity, helped contain the implications of basic principles. It was spirit that mattered.

Second, the obvious division between an abstract neo-scholasticism removed from life and the religious experience of Francis of Assisi seemed to confirm this insight. Latin syllogisms and the popular preaching of the friars were clearly uneasy partners. In the void left by the absence of a coherent intellectual tradition, the members of the family experienced a disconnection between their public neo-Thomism and their heartfelt devotion.

Third, within the contours of a moralized and separated religious life, the common life and the "spirit of Franciscan philosophy" as Boehner described it could meet only rarely in the extraordinary person who was able to combine criticism and obedience, freedom and regularity, theory and practice, progressive outreach with adherence to tradition. For most of us, the primacy of Christ meant devotion to the Sacred Heart and the Christmas crib; the distinct view of original sin translated into hymns in honor of Mary. Here, in images and song, the implications of the theology and praxis of Francis, Bonaventure, and Scotus could lie dormant and contained, communicated in a methodology of devotionalized pastoral presence, a "virtuous" way of being with the people. In these and other areas one could move to integrate spirit and life, soul and body, thought and structures, analysis and action, religious experience and intellectual reflection only at the expense of being accused of modernism and secularism.

The implications of Franciscan life and thought experienced containment in another area, that of the attitude of the members of the family to the social, political, and economic conditions of the world which surrounded them. Auweiler, as we have seen, hinted at some deeper connection between the Franciscan intellectual tradition and contemporary social problems, but the connections seemed attenuated. In his 1927 book, the Oxford professor C. R. S. Harris penned a brief exposition of Scotus's thinking on the origins of civil authority, the rooting of private property in positive law, the rejection of servitude as a natural state, usury, and the subordination of all economic activities to the "good of the community."[65]

For the most part, however, intellectual reflection on society, politics, and economics looked not toward the Franciscan notion of poverty—it had long since become domesticated away from its broader social implications—nor toward the dignity of the person so well articulated in Bonaventure, nor towards the principle of the social contract, nor towards Eden's perfect state of social communism.[66] Instead people recognized that the discrepancy between capital and labor was a social ill, that followers of the Saint of Assisi needed to engage themselves in the problems of the poor; but they saw these challenges from the perspective of the works of mercy and pastoral care. It is a startling fact that the two Educational Conferences held in the midst of the Depression (1934-1935), both of which were designed to address the social question, made little mention of particular Franciscan sources. The discourse on one of the great reformers, Bernardine of Siena, presented him as a great moral force not as a social prophet. Leo

---

[65]Harris, *Duns Scotus, I, The Place of Duns Scotus in Medieval Thought; II, The Philosophical Doctrines of Duns Scotus* (Oxford: Clarendon Press, MCMXXVII), with reference to II.345-357.

[66]Such a divorce from the concrete applications of life was helped of course by the philosophical and theological revival that looked toward the abstract essence of a school. It is notable that Gilson, in his flawed but important works (confer for example his "La Philosophie Franciscaine" as cited above), does not treat of Franciscan economic and social thought. Such reflection is notably missing also from Fr. James O'Mahony, "The Franciscan School of Philosophy." Conceptions of "philosophy" precluded a consideration of political economy.

XIII, Pius XI, and the institutionalized Thomism we have mentioned above dominated the discussions and shaped the economic critique. The internal forces of Americanization and the public fear of socialism prevented the consistent application of a "Franciscan economy" to the contemporary world.[67] The summary of the 1935 conference gave the overall rationale:[68]

> Studying the trends of our time, in sociology, economics, and politics; in religion, education and aesthetics, the Franciscan Educational Conference will base itself on the positive teaching of the Church as contained in the Gospels, in Christian Philosophy and in the Papal Decrees, and attempt to show how an application of Christian principles to everyday life is the real solution of the social evils so bitterly deplored by all thinking persons. And since the Popes have so frequently recommended the Third Order of St. Francis as containing all that is needed to reform the world, as loyal to the Popes we shall go on record as renewing our determination to work in season and out of season for the propagation of this ample means of reform.

The laity were invited to attend the 1935 conference so that a "frank exchange" between all parties could address the overwhelming problems. Three years later James Meyer published his *Social Ideals of St. Francis*. An admirable call for change, the exposition followed the usual pattern of an appeal to an idealized Francis, who gave up his prospects as a rich man's son to embrace "absolute poverty." Still, Meyer cautioned:

> Francis did not object to property, not even to money, on principle, any more than he objected on principle to the prevailing system of Feudalism or to the new mercantile aristocracy. In that precisely he differed from the doctrinaire

---

[67]See Cuthbert Gumbinger, O.F.M.Cap., "St. Bernardine of Siena, Model of Franciscan Social Activity," *Franciscan Educational Conference* XVII (1935), 1-7. For only one example of the adoption of Thomism see William Lavallee, O.F.M., "The Family, the Main Factor in Social Progress," *Franciscan Educational Conference* XVII (1935), 23-36. The Franciscan family followed the general contours of American Catholic thought as exemplified in David J. O'Brien, "The Economic Thought of the American Hierarchy," in Thomas Gannon, S.J., ed., *The Catholic Challenge to the American Economy* (New York: Macmillan, 1987), 27-41.
[68]See *Report of the Sixteenth Annual Meeting* and *Report of the Seventeenth Annual Meeting*, *Franciscan Educational Conference* XVI (November 1934), XVII (November 1935), with quotations from 1935.xx.

reformers of his day with their one sided conceptions of life and the mischief which ensued when they sought to give universal force to their unworkable theories.[69]

Here was a classic example of the difficulty of a "thought style" operating within a context of institutional amnesia.

By way of contrast, it was precisely during these same years that the new "social Catholicism" emerged not from within the Franciscan family but from such practitioners as Dorothy Day (1879-1980), Paul Hanley Furfey (1896-1992), and Catherine de Hueck Doherty (1896-1985).[70] It was they who drew inspiration from another type of Francis. On April 5, 1938, Virgil Michel, O.S.B., (1890-1938) spoke at Duns Scotus College on "The Liturgical Movement and the Franciscan Ideal." He argued for an "integrational life" between the world and God, body and soul, the individual and society. Michel noted three particular dimensions of the Franciscan ideal which were very contemporary in their application: (1) the material world as sharing in redemption through Christ; (2) seeing the divine in all things—sun, plants, animals—all of which were "quasi incarnations"; (3) seeing the divine in all people, so that one treated all like other Christs and one did all as Christ would do.[71]

Perhaps, the best indicator of the "institutional amnesia" that seemed to contain the family's full application of its own principles in the social and economic order came from a non-Catholic, Vida Dutton Scudder (1861-1954), the great Episcopalian social reformer who drew inspiration from the Franciscan tradition. She read the speeches from the 1934 Franciscan Educational Conference. Noting that the speakers constantly argued that Francis "was not concerned with economic or political issues," Scudder nevertheless saw a close connection between the authors' vows of poverty and their detachment from the *status quo*.

The essays abound in valuable concrete suggestions. They emphasize the unrealized possibilities of that Third Order so dear to Leo XIII; Fr. Hyacinth Ries, after fierce indictment of

---

[69]Fr. James Meyer, O.F.M., *Social Ideals of St. Francis: Eight Lessons in Applied Christianity* (St. Louis: B. Herder Book Co., 1938), 53.

[70]See for background Joseph P. Chinnici, O.F.M., Angelyn Dries, O.S.F., eds., *Prayer and Practice in the American Catholic Community* (Maryknoll, NY: Orbis Books, 2000), document 55, pp. 156-159.

[71]Virgil Michel, O.S.B., "Liturgical Movement and the Franciscan Ideal," in Virgil Michel Papers, Z-31, St. John's Abbey Archives, Collegeville, Minnesota.

the modern financial system, suggests that a Catholic parish might be its own banker! There is a plea for the introduction of social studies in the seminaries—it is pleasant to find a mandate for preparation of material to this end, in the Resolutions. The paper by Fr. Sylvester Brielmayer on moral theology urges, following Fr. Ryan, that discussion of obsolete issues in the Manuals be superceded by treatment of the Christian attitude toward such matters as "stock watering and its manifold causes; donations of tainted money; the lawful rate of profit on invested capital; boycott, strikes, laborers, copyright, and patent." Reminiscent of old Franciscan debates on "*Usus*" and "*Dominium*" is the emphasis on growing domination by wealth rather than on profit, as spiritually the most dangerous feature in our present situation.[72]

If the friars did not recognize the deeper roots of their heritage, Scudder certainly did! Speaking as a radical, she held out an olive branch of alliance and also went to the heart of the internal problem of amnesia:

> In common with all his confreres, Fr. Tschippert of course accepts the official Roman view of the "inviolability of private property"; but no Communist need feel remote from a position which leads the friars, following the Holy Father, to search for a remedy to "the maldistribution of wealth" by determining "the boundaries imposed by the requirements of social life upon the right to ownership itself or upon its use."[73]

As much as I can determine, the Franciscan family in the United States, following the lead of the Church and in concert with many other American Catholics, began to break free from both the shadow of neo-Thomism and the context of containment in the period following World War II. This era would see a growing awareness of the inherited deficiencies of the theological, ecclesial, and pedagogical boundaries of thought. The European religious leadership of Pacificus Perantoni

---

[72]Vida Dutton Scudder as quoted in *Franciscan Educational Conference* XVII (1935), xii, which cites a review of Scudder's in *Living Church* (March 23, 1935).
[73]*Franciscan Educational Conference* XVII (1935), xiii. On Scudder's Franciscan affinities, see her classic book *The Franciscan Adventure: A Study in the First Hundred Years of the Order of St. Francis of Assisi* (New York: E. P. Dutton & Co., 1931); Stephen Cavin, "The Politics of Empathy: Vida Scudder on the Early Franciscans and the Rudiments of Social Reform," M. A. Thesis, Graduate Theological Union, 1986.

(1947-1951) and the shift occurring in Franciscan scholarship itself began the overall move away from the structures of containment. Social development and religious life began to be interrelated.[74] The work of Dominican scholars broke open the historical limitations of the "mentality of Christendom" and related the thirteenth century reform movements more and more to their lay constituents.[75]

In the United States the first comprehensive essay on Scotus's social thought, done not by a philosopher but by a sociologist, appears to have been published in 1951.[76] The religious men began to open up new ministries in response to the rapid social mutations occurring throughout the Catholic community.[77] The women participating in the Sister Formation Conference, helped by the friars, pushed for the integration of thought and life, piety and learning, theory and structures.[78] One wonders whether or not at least some people were trying to make a statement with the publication of Bonaventure's *De Reductione Artium ad Theologiam* in 1955. According to the editors:

> The Seraphic Doctor was addressing academicians. He was speaking of the different departments and sciences of the University program. Hence, his immediate purpose was to show the organic connection between the departments of Arts

---

[74]See for example, Perantoni, "Divina Providentia," 2 Augusti 1947, in R. P. Albertus Ghinato, O.F.M., ed., *Enchiridion Vitae Franciscanae, Excerpta ex Actis Ministrorum Generalium, O.F.M. (1897-1957)*, II (Quarrachi-Florentiae: Collegii S. Bonaventurae, 1957), 38-89, for the new apostolic urgency. For the changing scholarship in the post-War period, see Grado G. Merlo, "La Storiografia Francescana dal DopoGuerra ad Oggi," in Francesco Santi, ed., *Gli Studi Francescana dal Dopoguerra ad Oggi* (Spoleto: Studi sull'Alto Medioevo, 1993), 3-32.

[75]Most notable of course were Chenu and Congar. For purposes of this essay see Yves Congar, O.P., "St. Francis of Assisi: or the Gospel as an Absolute in Christendom," first given in 1952 and republished in Maurice W. Sheehan, O.F.M.Cap., ed., *St. Francis of Assisi: Essays in Commemoration, 1982* (St. Bonaventure, NY: The Franciscan Institute, 1982), 59-76; M.-D. Chenu, *La théologie au douzieme siècle* (Paris: J. Vring 1957), which was selected, edited, and translated by Jerome Taylor and Lester K. Little in *Nature, Man, and Society in the Twelfth Century: Essays on New Theological Perspectives in the Latin West* (Chicago: The University of Chicago Press, 1968). See especially the chapter on "The Evangelical Awakening."

[76]Anthony Soto, O.F.M., "The Structure of Society according to John Duns Scotus," *Franciscan Studies*, 11 (1951): 194-212; 12 (1952): 71-90.

[77]For one example see Joseph P. Chinnici, O.F.M., "Fidelity and Change: Historical Reflections on Change in the Province of Saint Barbara, 1915-1976," unpublished mss. in author's possession, 2000.

[78]See Angelyn Dries, O.S.F., "Living in Ambiguity: A Paradigm Shift Experienced by the Sister Formation Movement," *Catholic Historical Review*, LXXIX (July 1993): 478-487; Marjorie Noterman Beane, *From Framework to Freedom: A History of the Sister Formation Conference* (Lanham, MD: University Press of America, 1993).

and Theology; in fact, to prove scientifically that the arts or all secular studies must be grouped under theology; that theology is the unifying and clarifying science of all the other sciences; that no philosophical knowledge is complete and adequate unless it is studied in the light of theological truth.[79]

When the renewal came with its full institutional force in the 1960s, it would dissolve the structures of containment by reshaping both the Church's relationship with the world and the very description of "the universal call to holiness." The "spirit of Franciscan philosophy," no longer constrained by its definition of religious life nor by its antipathy towards systemic social criticism and engagement, would finally be granted institutional permission to find its own body. The ministries and conventual life of all religious would be thrown into disarray and with it the way in which they thought about themselves. It would take some time. From the renewal chapters of 1967-1968 to the Third Order Regular "Response to the Lineamenta" of 1994, which officially articulated the charism of the Franciscan Evangelical Life, historical memory, confined to the unconscious, emerged only slowly into the public marketplace.[80] But during this time, as we have noted above, the very structures that would support a conscious mobilization of resources would disappear. No longer contained by the forces of an institutional amnesia, the charism would first have to rebuild itself and then become self-conscious and establish some coherence between life and thought, between aspirations and structures, before it could even consider achieving a public presence. And that is where we come in.

Mobilizing Our Resources: A Strategic Revival

Theology is enmeshed in history. It is always implicated in strategic pastoral choice. It is only by obfuscation that theology can be called, in any multiple sense, a-historical or a-cultural. Even a-historical orthodoxy, to use Michael Novak's descriptive phrase for post-Tridentine Catholic theology,

[79]Philotheus Boehner, O.F.M., and M. Frances Laughlin, S.M.I.C., *Works of Saint Bonaventure, Volume I* (Saint Bonaventure, NY: The Franciscan Institute, 1955), 18. Volume II on the *Itinerarium Mentis in Deum* followed in 1956.
[80]See The Sisters and Brothers of the T.O.R., "Response to the *Lineamenta*," *The Cord*, 44 (November 1994): 289-291; see in the same issue Joseph P. Chinnici, O.F.M., "The Prophetic Heart: The Evangelical Form of Religious Life in the United States," 292-306.

contains implicit strategic decisions for Church-society relationships. Every theology is a strategic theology.[81]

I have tried in the preceding remarks to situate our retrieval of the Franciscan intellectual tradition, especially its theological tendencies, within the context of a long twentieth-century quest. It is clear, I hope, from this overview, that previous retrievals have been strategic, shaped in large part by the forces of the pre-conciliar Church. Choices have been made in response to ecclesial, intellectual, and political-economic developments. These in turn have shaped our discourse and understanding of the tradition itself. The key marks of the retrieval have become apparent:

- its major differences from official neo-Thomism;
- its need to defend its orthodoxy in the face of attacks from the intransigent parties in the Church;
- its conception of itself as an abstract coherent whole, with a set profile and essential elements;
- its divorce of theology from the roots of communal religious life;
- its separation as an autonomous discipline from the dynamism of social, economic, and political change;
- its containment through the exaltation of its founder and the images and practices of popular religiosity;
- its fracturing of the unity between religious experience, intellectual reflection, communal life, and mission.

Within this historical context, we can also identify clearly how vital were our predecessors in terms of exposing central features of the tradition, establishing and translating critical texts, rebuilding our knowledge, so to speak, from the ground up, penetrating the philosophy, upholding standards of scholarship, and practicing the central virtues.

The socio-cultural mutation brought on by the 1960s, what Chenu referred to as the "end of the Constantinian era," and the changes initiated by the Second Vatican Council revealed the faultlines that ran

---

[81]John A. Coleman, *An American Strategic Theology* (New York/Ramsey: Paulist Press, 1982), 131-132.

through these pre-conciliar developments.[82] We can now see this effort's refusal of development and history, its failure to take into account its own diversity, its tendency to deny the value of personal religious experience. At the same time, these same changes opened up to us the possibility of analyzing the tradition as it emerged out of history and developed from a continual dialogue with change.[83] We have, to some extent, been able to break free of the institutional memory that shaped past interpretations. Because of our own "return to the charism," we have discovered a new hope of linking communal religious life, intellectual formulation, spiritual practices, and pastoral strategies. While Francis, Bonaventure, Olivi, Scotus, and Ockham are all now becoming demythologized, we ourselves are being given the possibilities of a new institutional discourse that can integrate the intellectual patrimony with our own heartfelt inspirations as Franciscans. We are clearly in the midst of a contemporary revival of both Bonaventure and Scotus.[84] The issue of making these new insights popularly available still eludes us. All of this is shaping and encouraging our project on the Retrieval of the Franciscan Intellectual Tradition.

From my perspective as an historian, how we go about this retrieval, how we now mobilize our dwindling resources needs to be shaped by the history I have outlined here. The lights and shadows of

---

[82]M.-D.Chenu, "Le fin de l'ère constantienne," in *Un Concile pour notre temps* (Paris: Editions du Cerf, 1961), 59-88.

[83]Fundamental starting points are Roberto Lambertini, Andrea Tabarroni, *Dopo Francesco: L'Eredità Difficile* (Torino: Edizioni Gruppo Ebele, 1989); and the articles in *Dalla "Sequela Christi" di Francesco d'Assisi all'Apologia della Povertà, Atti del XVIII Covegno Internazionale di studi francescani, Assisi, 18-20 Ottobre, 1990* (Spoleto: Centro italiano di studi sull'Alto Medioevo, 1992).

[84]The retrieval of the tradition, its continuity with Francis, needs to be considered in the light of the considerable historical work being done on Francis himself. Most notable is the work that places him in the context of the lay evangelical reform. Fundamental are Giovanni Miccoli, "Francis of Assisi's Christian Proposal," *Greyfriars Review*, 3 (1989): 127-172, and Chiara Frugoni, *Francis of Assisi* (London: SCM Press, 1998, with American edition also). See for just some accessible examples on Bonaventure and Scotus, Zachary Hayes, *The Hidden Center: Spirituality and Speculative Christology in St. Bonaventure* (NY: Paulist Press, 1981, republished by the Franciscan Institute); Ilia Delio, O.S.F., *Crucified Love: Bonaventure's Mysticism of the Crucified Christ* (Quincy, IL: Franciscan Press, 1998); Timothy Johnson, ed., *Bonaventure: Mystic of God's Word* (New York: New City Press, 1999); Richard Cross, *Duns Scotus* (New York: Oxford University Press, 1999); Mary Beth Ingham, C.S.J., *The Harmony of Goodness: Mutuality and Moral Living According to John Duns Scotus* (Quincy, IL: Franciscan Press, 1996); Thomas A. Shannon, *The Ethical Theory of John Duns Scotus* (Quincy, IL: Franciscan Press, 1995); Allan B. Wolter, O.F.M., Blane O'Neill, O.F.M., *John Duns Scotus: Mary's Architect* (Quincy, IL: Franciscan Press, 1993). For an overview that treats the Franciscan school seriously, see G. R. Evans, ed., *The Medieval Theologians: An Introduction to Theology in the Medieval Period* (Oxford: Blackwell Publishers, 2001).

the pre-conciliar period influence the knowledge and confusion that we now experience. In addition, the dissolution of the infrastructure that supported the colleges, educational conferences, publications, and communal character of our former identity has left us with no coherent sense of ourselves, our formation programs, our ministries, or our pastoral practice. We have few organs of communication that reach the places where we meet the people and their concerns meet us. Yet our experience of the last thirty-five years has also shown us part of the path. We are now at the point where we must either articulate the intellectual inheritance by updating it into new forms of life, thought, and communication, or we will lose it, and with it, ourselves. Patricia Wittberg has identified the following elements as essential preconditions for the recovery of a coherent social and public identity at the present time, all of which will need to be present in our current endeavor:

(1) the development of a common discourse of memory and rituals;
(2) the ability to make a "frame alignment" for the interpretation of our culture, i.e. update it;
(3) the mobilization of our resources of recruitment, finances, networks, and alliance with authority;
(4) the development of communal commitment mechanisms, such as common stories, rituals, definitions of boundaries, shared commitment to sacrifice.[85]

In the light of this and in conclusion, let me indicate the following points, both areas of mobilization and also "guiding principles" so to speak, which I place before you in hopes of dialogue and development. They emerge, I believe, from the initiatives we have now begun and the history I have tried to elucidate.

---

[85]Patricia Wittberg, S.C., *The Rise and Decline of Catholic Religious Orders: A Social Movement Perspective* (Albany, NY: State University of New York Press, 1994), Chapter 2.

Areas of Mobilization

The Implementation of a Strategic Plan

Our own diminishment has opened up to us the urgency of the coordination of efforts and the importance of networking to revitalize our Franciscan intellectual inheritance. A strategic plan, referred to at the beginning of this paper, has been developed over the past year. As a starting point, the English Speaking Conference, Order of Friars Minor, has established a five-year Commission on the Franciscan Intellectual Tradition (CFIT). Hopefully, this Commission will broaden itself to be representative of all the dimensions of our family. The plan itself must be phased into being. Although presented as an integrated approach, we know that it will remain disparate. (In our Franciscan universe, all things are creaturely, contingent!) We do not see this as simply an initiative of the English Speaking Conference. In fact, it can hardly succeed without the expertise and skill of the members of the Franciscan Federation and other dimensions of the First and Second Orders. The North American Capuchin Conference has already offered its support. Hopefully, the CFIT will have its first official meeting in fall 2001 and an extended planning meeting in January 2002.

Networking and the Coordination of Efforts

As much as possible, we should try to build on the structures that currently exist, using local resources to network in a new way and to present a common program of articulation. Currently, the CFIT would like to work with and network with various local initiatives to see what is possible:

* The Annual Forum at the Washington Theological Union
* The Colorado Springs Forum on Franciscan Life and Themes
* The Association of Franciscan Colleges and Universities
* The Academy of American Franciscan History

CFIT would also like to begin some new initiatives:

- Explore the possibility of establishing an International English Speaking Academy of Franciscan Scholars
- Establish a national website linking various local initiatives and providing information and popular resources for the Franciscan Intellectual Tradition
- Establish a Forum of Exchange between the Franciscan Institute, the Franciscan Study Centre, Washington Theological Union, Chicago Theological Union, and the Franciscan School of Theology, Berkeley
- Organize a meeting of representatives from Franciscan publishing houses associated with the English Speaking Conference
- Begin meeting with formators of the English Speaking Conference so as to develop programs for initial and ongoing formation

A Program of Intellectual Articulation

We would like to begin exploring and articulating a contemporary understanding of the Franciscan Intellectual Tradition in many of its dimensions. Initiatives here will vary a great deal.

- A working document has already been prepared in the area of key theological concepts. It is a discussion piece and is meant to be modified and corrected. In some areas, for example, ecclesiology and evangelization, there is need for much further exploration.
- A great deal remains to be done in fields that are not just theological. Some specific areas, for example, are the history of the entire family (particularly in the post-Reformation period) and a new cultural history that relates high theology with mysticism, popular religiosity, missiology, art, and the work of women.
- There is need for a basic outline of key ideas and principles that have contemporary application; for example, a systematic reflection by scholars willing to interface the tradition with the

complexities of contemporary cultural and ecclesial life; social and sexual ethics; inter-religious and inter-faith dialogue; pastoral practice; the understanding of poverty; the virtues necessary for inter-cultural living.

- Finally, on a popular level, we need to develop organs of communication (pamphlets, workbooks, homily helps, etc.) and pools of writers that can assist on a wider basis to disseminate a new vision in pastoral work, preaching, moral discernment, spiritual direction, the development of a coherent philosophy of formation, etc. The meetings and gatherings outlined above can be opportunities to explore these possibilities.

At the moment, there are hopes to use the annual gatherings in Washington, Colorado Springs, the summer school at the Franciscan Institute, and a history forum planned for Fall 2003 to develop these areas further. CFIT will continue to explore and develop two specific content areas:

- A working paper on the Franciscan Intellectual Tradition
- The development of a basic Catechism

Some Guiding Principles

1. The isolation of disciplines one from another has been a real difficulty in the history I have outlined here. Philosophy and theology, economics and politics, history and science, spirituality and liturgy have all developed as autonomous disciplines within our educational traditions. In many respects, this has been good as each has its own requirements for verification. However, my impression today is that our younger people no longer think in this fashion; the boundaries between the disciplines need to be respected but they also need to be bridged. For example, we can no longer imagine a theology that does not interface in some way with the natural, human, and social sciences. As much as possible, the gatherings mentioned above should try to facilitate dialogue and integration between heretofore autonomous modes of thought.

2. For historic and cultural reasons, the history I have examined deals almost entirely with men and clerics well trained in the tradition. Today we are newly aware of gender issues, diverse learning styles, and moral decision-making processes. We have greater understanding of the Franciscan family, its shared charism, and the ecclesial need to relate lay and religious, men and women to each other. The initiatives we undertake need to witness to a communal intellectual endeavor of far-reaching inclusiveness. Just as theological sources must no longer be confined to scholastic texts but encompass the witnesses of our spiritual tradition, so also men and women, clergy and laity need to work together if our Franciscan tradition is to have a public presence suited to the twenty-first century. Vital to the retrieval will be our ability to network with our lay colleagues in colleges and universities.

3. The new studies of Francis of Assisi and the first hundred years of the tradition firmly locate our intellectual reality within the context of the political, social, cultural, and economic currents of the thirteenth century.[86] We are more aware than ever that Bonaventure's intellectual program was related to currents within the Order and the Church. Olivi's thinking can hardly be divorced from his ecclesiology, concern for the practice of poverty, and lay spiritual direction. Scotus's approach in an abstract treatise such as *De Primo Principio* "is a singularly successful attempt to bring study and prayer together."[87] All of this indicates that the intellectual program enunciated by the leaders in the schools emerged from the formational ideals, pastoral practices, and social settings of their own day. Theirs

---

[86]See as two examples Jacques LeGoff, *Saint François d'Assise* (Paris: Gallimard, 1999), with the collection of his classic articles; Odd Langholm, *Economics in the Medieval Schools: Wealth, Exchange, Value, Money and Usury according to the Paris Theological Tradition 1200-1350* (Leiden: E. J. Brill, 1992). I have tried to address the implications of some of these studies in "Poverty: An Image for the Franciscan Presence in the World," *Laurentianum* 41 (2000): 413-437.

[87]See Dominic Monti, O.F.M., *St. Bonaventure's Writings concerning the Franciscan Order: Works of Saint Bonavneture*, V (St. Bonaventure, NY: The Franciscan Institute, 1994), general editor George Marcil, O.F.M; for Olivi see the studies in Raoul Manselli, *Da Gioacchino da Fiore a Cristoforo Colombo, Studi sull' Francescanesimo Spirituale sull'Ecclesiologica e sull'Escatologismo Bassomedievali*, a cura di Paolo Vian (Roma: Institute Palazzo Borromini, 1997), 345-365, 109-128; Robert P. Prentice, *The Basic Quidditative Metaphysics of Duns Scotus as Seen in His* De Primo Principio (Roma: Antonianum, 1970), quotation from page 195.

was a strategic theology. An intuition and experience of God took shape from the cultural and religious context that history and God's grace gave to people. Chenu's definition of theology takes on complete relevance here: It is a spirituality that finds rational instruments adequate to its religious experience.

4. Such a perspective means that we can no longer isolate our philosophical and theological inheritance from our structures of formation and our concrete experience of a God-centered life in the tradition of Francis and Clare. Our social location, our option for the poor, our ability to stand together between the margins of the Church and the margins of society, our conversion towards the Gospel itself—these areas are the specific environment from which our theological and intellectual reflection takes life. The tradition itself emerges from the marginal experience of poverty, and it is only when we actively engage both our life and our mission that our intellectual reflection takes on its truly creative heart. I cannot emphasize enough that the retrieval of our tradition is yoked to our willingness to embody our evangelical life form as a viable religious life in the Church and in society.

Such an integration of life and thought, body and spirit, experience and reflection within the context of our evangelical call will necessarily lead to some conflict both within society and the Church. Here we must act carefully and take seriously Francis's admonition of "being Catholic." The position from which we reflect necessarily entails both a self-discipline of respect and loyalty to the hierarchy and a "being with the other," who remains by definition outside of the care of the institutional Church. The history we have examined indicates that because of this positioning and some of its fundamental philosophical and theological beliefs (e.g. the univocity of being, a focus on the will and charity, the absolute freedom of God, the primacy of Christ, the moral focus on intentionality and personalism) the Franciscan intellectual tradition has either been merely tolerated or overtly condemned in many circles in the Church of the modern era. It would be naïve to think that *Fides et Ratio*, the recent papal encyclical that again emphasized the inheritance of Thomism and merely mentions other traditions of thought, will not be used by some to curtail the public presence of other modes of thinking and pastoral action.[88] The question is: Will we be up to the task of retrieving the Franciscan tradition from within the experience of marginality? Only if, I believe, we root ourselves at the same time deeply in the primacy of the Trinity and its sacramental and hidden expression in the world, including the institutional Church.

---

[88]See *Fides et Ratio* (57-63) printed in *Origins*, 28 (October 22, 1998).

Authors

Margaret Carney, O.S.F., is a member of the Sisters of St. Francis of the Providence of God, Pittsburgh, Pennsylvania, whom she served for eight years as general minister. She received her doctorate at the Pontificium Athenaeum Antonianum in Rome. From 1994-96, she chaired the LCWR task force on Leadership Roles for Women in the Church. Having served as a faculty member at The Franciscan Institute, St. Bonaventure University, St. Bonaventure, New York, from 1998-1999, she became Director of the Institute and Dean of the Franciscan Studies program on June 1, 1999. She is a member of the Franciscan Pilgrimage staff and author of *The First Franciscan Woman, Clare of Assisi & Her Form of Life* (Franciscan Press, 1993).

Joseph Chinnici, O.F.M., earned his D.Phil. in ecclesiastical history from Oxford University. A professor of history at the Franciscan School of Theology in Berkeley, California, he is the author of *Living Stones: the History and Structure of Catholic Spiritual Life in the United States* (Macmillan, 1988). He has also taught occasional courses at the Franciscan Institute, St. Bonaventure University. A member of the Province of St. Barbara, Oakland, California, he served as Provincial Minister for a number of years. At the helm of the revival of the Franciscan intellectual tradition, he is especially interested in a contemporary understanding of the evangelical life. He presently serves as Dean of Studies at the Franciscan School of Theology, Berkeley.

Vincent Cushing, O.F.M., is a friar of Holy Name Province, New York. He served for twenty-four years as president of Washington Theological Union (1975-1999) and remains part of the faculty as assistant professor in the department of systematic theology. He also serves as Director of Keystone Seminary Associates, a service to American Catholic seminaries of the National Catholic Education Association, and is a research fellow of the Louisville Institute of Louisville Presbyterian Seminary. He is currently writing a book on post-conciliar seminary education.

Ilia Delio, O.S.F., a member of the Franciscan Servants of the Holy
Child Jesus, North Plainfield, New Jersey, did her doctoral studies in
theology at Fordham University. She is presently at Washington
Theological Union, Washington, DC, serving as an assistant professor
of ecclesial history and Franciscan studies and as Director of the
Franciscan Center. She is a visiting professor at The Franciscan
Institute, St. Bonaventure, New York. She is author of *Crucified Love:
Bonaventure's Mysticism of the Crucified Christ* (Quincy: Franciscan Press,
1998) and *Simply Bonaventure: An Introduction to His Life, Thought, and
Writings* (New York: New City Press, 2001).

Zachary Hayes, O.F.M., is a friar of the Sacred Heart Province, St.
Louis. He earned his doctorate at the University of Bonn, Germany. He
has been a professor of historical and systematic theology at Catholic
Theological Union, Chicago, since 1968. A noted Bonaventure scholar,
he is a past recipient of the John Courtney Murray Award of the
Catholic Theological Society of America. He is author of *The Hidden
Center: Spirituality and Speculative Christology in St. Bonaventure* (St.
Bonaventure, NY: The Franciscan Institute, 1992). He has contributed
translations to the *Works of Saint Bonaventure* series of the Franciscan
Institute: Vol. III, *Disputed Questions on the Trinity*, 1979, and Vol. IV,
On the Knowledge of Christ, 1992. He also wrote a chapter on
Bonaventure in the *History of Franciscan Theology* (St. Bonaventure, NY:
The Franciscan Institute, 1994). His latest book is *The Gift of Being: A
Theology of Creation* (Collegeville, MN: Liturgical Press, 2001).

Mary Elizabeth Ingham, C.S.J., is a Sister of St. Joseph of Orange,
California. She taught for a number of years in secondary eduction and
in 1987 received her Ph.D. from the University of Fribourg,
Switzerland. Since then she has taught philosophy at Loyola
Marymount University, where she is currently Chair of the Department
of Philosophy. She has published several articles on Scotus and a book,
*The Harmony of Goodness: Mutuality and Moral Living according to John
Duns Scotus* (Franciscan Press, 1996).

Dominic Monti, O.F.M., is a friar of Holy Name Province, New York. He received his Ph.D. at the University of Chicago, where he studied under Bernard McGinn. He has taught at Washington Theological Union since 1979 in the Department of Ecclesiastical History and is Chair of the department. In 1994, he contributed translations of Bonaventure's *Writings Concerning the Franciscan Order* as part of the *Works of Saint Bonaventure* series, Vol. V (St. Bonaventure, NY: The Franciscan Institute). He made significant contributions to *Francis of Assisi: Early Documents* (New York: New City Press, 1999-2001). He is presently finishing a new translation of Bonaventure's *Breviloquium.*

Kenan B. Osborne, O.F.M., is a friar of the St. Barbara Province, Oakland, California. He did his higher studies at the University of Munich and has taught systematic theology at the Franciscan School of Theology, Berkeley, since 1967, specializing in ecclesiology and sacramental theology. He is presently professor emeritus there. He was recipient of the Franciscan Medal from the Franciscan Institute in 1999. In 1994 he edited *The History of Franciscan Theology* (St. Bonaventure, NY: The Franciscan Institute), contributing a chapter on Alexander of Hales. His most recent publication is *Christian Sacraments in a Postmodern World: A Theology for the Third Millenium* (New York: Paulist Press, 1999). His current special interest is inter-religious dialogue.

Diane Tomkinson, O.S.F., a graduate of Swarthmore College, has been a member of the Sisters of St. Francis of Philadelphia (Aston) since 1983. She served in campus ministry in the Archdiocese of Philadelphia and parish ministry in Phoenixville, Pennsylvania, Wilmington, Delaware, and Lake City, South Carolina. She received her master's degree in theology from Washington Theological Union in 1994 and is currently a doctoral candidate in historical theology at Fordham University. She has presented papers on early Franciscan women at the 1999 College Theology Society Convention and at the International Medieval Conference in Kalamazoo, Michigan (2000 and 2001). Her dissertation is on Angela of Foligno as a vernacular theologian and on Angela's Trinitarian Theology.